CW00407518

On The Trail Of Robin Hood

by
Richard de Vries

Revised and illustrated
by
Paul W. Cullen and Rodney Hordern

Crossbow Books

First published by Archaeology in Education, 1982.

This revised and expanded edition published by Crossbow Books, Hightown L38 9EP.

ISBN 1 869823 02 8

Second Impression 1989

Acknowledgements
We are grateful for the help given by Graham Black, senior curator of Nottingham Castle Museum, Mr K Hordern and Mrs L Sharp.

CONTENTS

LIST OF ILLUSTRATIONS

1. Outlaws at Wentbridge.
2. Early woodcut depicting Robin Hood.
3. Henry II.
4. Edward I.
5. Map showing the distribution of Robin Hood place names.
6. The medieval greenwood.
7. Map of Sherwood Forest.
8. Map of Barnsdale.
9. Bird's eye view of Wentbridge and Saylis.
10. Tomb of Robin Hood.
11. The Sheriff.
12. Little John's grave slab.
13. The thirteenth century windmill.
14. The thirteenth century knight.
15. Women's dress in the thirteenth century.
16. The Betley window (8V0 P149 LINC. The Bodleian Library).
17. Steetley chapel.
18. St. Mary's Abbey, York.
19. Kirklees Priory.
20. Little John's cottage at Hathersage.
21. Robin Hood's Cross, Derbyshire.
22. Nottingham Castle.
23. King John's Palace.
24. A thirteenth century fortified manor house.
25. Royal Forests of the thirteenth century.
26. Hunting the red deer.
27. The red deer.
28. The longbowman.
29. Map of Wentbridge.
30. Robin Hood's Well.
31. Burghwallis Church.
32. Little John's Well.
33. Pontefract Castle.
34. Robin Hood.
35. The Major Oak.
36. The guest house at Kirkstall Abbey.
37. Clitheroe Castle.
38. Lee in Wyresdale.
39. Clifford's Tower, York. (© Historic Buildings and Monuments Commission for England).
40. Gatehouse of St. Mary's Abbey at York.
41. Map of Yorkshire, Nottinghamshire and Derbyshire.
42. Map of Lancashire.

All illustrations not acknowledged are by Rodney Hordern.

INTRODUCTION

The Story of Robin Hood

The name, and exploits, of Robin Hood are known throughout most of the world. In his life-story as it is known today, he lived in the reign of Richard I – Richard the Lionheart – at the close of the twelfth century, and his headquarters were deep in the Forest of Sherwood. From here, helped by a large band of 'merry men', he robbed the rich to help the poor, and carried on a persistent guerilla war against the Sheriff of Nottingham. Born in Loxley, and heir to the title Earl of Huntingdon, Robin wooed and married the Lady Marian, a royal ward, and was at length pardoned by the king – to whom he had always sworn his loyalty – and was even taken into the kings service. Eventually, however, he returned to live in the forest and finally met his death at the treacherous hands of his kinswoman, the prioress of Kirklees. Some place his death in the year 1247.

The purpose of this publication is to present the evidence for Robin Hood and his activities, by taking the reader on a journey back to the earliest known origins of the legend, and to see, if it is possible to separate fact from fiction.

(fig. 1) Outlaws at Wentbridge
By the thirteenth century much of England was owned by the monastic houses whose abbots and priors abused their position. It is clear from the 'Gest' that Robin Hood singled out such institutions as 'fair game'; indeed monks and canons were often subject to attack and robbery.

THE AGE OF ROBIN HOOD

The Evidence
The Ballads

The story of Robin Hood as recounted is the end product of centuries of additions and alterations, and therefore in searching for Robin Hood it is necessary to examine the original medieval source material, including ballads which were recited to audiences. There are altogether some thirty eight ballads of Robin Hood, not all are medieval in origin, and others were modified after the Middle

(fig. 2) Early Woodcut of Robin Hood
Once the stories of Robin Hood were in print, illustrations were sought to embellish them and the early printers satisfied themselves by delving into their store of woodcuts. This picture may previously have been used in several unrelated works.

Ages, but they all represent the prime source of evidence for Robin Hood.

The nature of the ballads

To judge how far we can rely on the evidence of the ballads as sources for information about an historical Robin Hood, it is first necessary to understand what were the ballads and how they have developed.

Late medieval references to the story of Robin Hood speak of 'rymes', 'songs', 'fables and jestes', and there can be no doubt that the various adventures of the legendary outlaw were recounted orally time and time again in most parts of Britain in the fifteenth century. The fact that we call these stories 'ballads' is perhaps misleading, for it is by no means certain that most of them were sung to their audiences. It seems more likely that many were recited. In any event, the fact that the stories were told orally inevitably means that they must have suffered many changes of detail during the early centuries of their existence as the entertainers who told them made their own additions and alterations to make the stories more dramatic, more appealing, or better suited to their particular audience. The ballads as they survive must be used with great care, but they do provide clues as to the time and place in which any historical figure behind the legend may have lived.

The written versions of the ballads have themselves gone through a similar process to that experienced by the oral versions. Most of the copies or manuscripts which survive reveal clear evidence that they have been copies from earlier written versions, and sometimes it is possible to see that two or three different versions have been amalgamated into one. We must therefore recognise that the original ballads or stories of Robin Hood have undergone considerable alteration over a period of several centuries.

1. The date of the ballads

Only three of all the ballads of Robin Hood survive in copies, written down as early as 1500. The earliest of these is probably the manuscript copy of the story of *Robin Hood and the Monk*, which was produced in the mid-fifteenth century. Next in date perhaps, is the story of *Robin Hood and the Potter*, which survives in a manuscript of around 1500. It is possible, nevertheless, that the most famous (and longest) of all the Robin Hood stories – *A Gest of Robyn Hode* – is slightly earlier. Two printed versions of this story survive, one published probably around 1510, the other sometime in the years between 1492 and 1534.

It must be remembered that these dates refer only to the age of the oldest surviving copies of these stories – not to the age of the stories or ballads themselves. These are clearly much older, and we find several clues which allow us to trace the ballads back further into the medieval period. The two versions of the *Gest* are so similar that it is believed that there must have been a standardized version circulating in the fifteenth century; more important still, experts agree that the language of the *Gest* points to the whole ballad having been put together as a single story by the turn of the fourteenth century. We can detect these separate stories, each of which contains more than one tale or has been put together itself from more than one version. Therefore, these original stories must themselves date back well before 1400.

Similarly, some of the ballads, (of which the earliest surviving texts date as late as the 1760's), can be shown to have existed much earlier. The story of *Robin Hoode his Death*, for example, was clearly known at the time when the versions of the *Gest* were printed around 1500, for they summarise an account of his death which is very similar to that in the *Gest*. Equally, the story of *Robin Hood and Guy of Gisbourne* is already found in a fragment of a play, written down around 1475. There are then, a group of ballads whose medieval origins are quite certain and assured.

2. Other documents

Apart from the ballads of Robin Hood, there are a number of other documents which we can use in trying to seek at least the outlines of historical truth (if any) contained within the ballads. Three fifteenth century Scottish chroniclers, for example, all refer to Robin Hood as a historical character – they at least had no doubts that he had existed. Other references to Robin Hood include a lawsuit of 1429, and a petition to Parliament dated some ten years later, but it is not clear from these brief references whether he was regarded as a purely legendary figure known only from popular ballads or as a real person. Into the same category must fall a popular fifteenth century proverb – "Many speak of Robin Hood that never bent his bow" – and the earliest of all references to Robin Hood, in the poem of *Piers Plowman*, dated around 1377. This refers, in somewhat disparaging terms, to 'rymes of Robyn

(fig. 3) Henry III
Henry succeeded King John in 1216 and reigned for 56 years. Although his era was one of economic expansion and saw the foundation of the modern parliament, it was also an age of disorder and widespread banditry.

Hood', but the disparagement is of the disreputable or ribald nature of the 'rymes', not of Robin Hood's historical reality – on which no comment is offered.

So far, we have looked at the sources which clearly refer to the Robin Hood – outlaw and opponent of the Sheriff. There are other documents, several of them, which refer to various Robin Hoods, who actually lived between 1200 and 1400. These are mainly local documents, concerned with the law or with land-holding, which have survived and are today stored in archives. It is clearly amongst these that we will have to search for any possible historical Robin Hood that we might equate to the hero of the legends. But did that hero really exist, or was he just a romantic figment of the balladeer's imagination?

Robin Hood: fact or fiction?

In trying to answer this question, it must be said at once that there is certainly no clear historical evidence that the Robin Hood of the legend was a real person – obviously if such documentary evidence existed, there would be no need to ask the question. But of course, the same is true of other famous figures in history, such as King Arthur. On the other hand, if we look at the other legendary outlaws, such as Billy the Kid, Jesse James and Ned Kelly – all of whom had similarly 'robbed the rich to help the poor' stories woven around them – we find that they existed and are historically documented. But they, of course, had the benefit of living in more recent times than those to which any historical Robin Hood might belong, and documentary evidence of their existence is therefore, more likely to have survived. One might still argue, however, that if Robin Hood was really as famous throughout England as the medieval ballads suggest, there should surely be some clear reference to his outlaw activities in contemporary court records.

There are three points which together suggest that Robin Hood was probably a real historical figure. First, and least significant, is the point that many of the episodes recorded in the ballads of Robin Hood certainly occurred – not just once but many times – in medieval England. Outlaws did infest the forest, particularly along the road to the North, they did take the king's deer, and sheriffs certainly oppressed the peasant farmers and practised extortion and terror. Secondly, although the ballads and narrative tales of the Middle Ages were meant as entertainment, they were also regarded as

(fig. 4) Edward I
He came to the throne in 1272 and began military campaigns against Wales and Scotland. He may have been the Edward referred to in the 'Gest'.

popular history. Finally, the earliest stories of Robin Hood all seem to point very clearly indeed to a very specific part of northern England as the setting of the stories – so specific, and in some ways so surprising – that it is hard to believe they refer to some idealised or symbolic character rather than to historical reality.

(fig. 5) Robin Hood Place Names

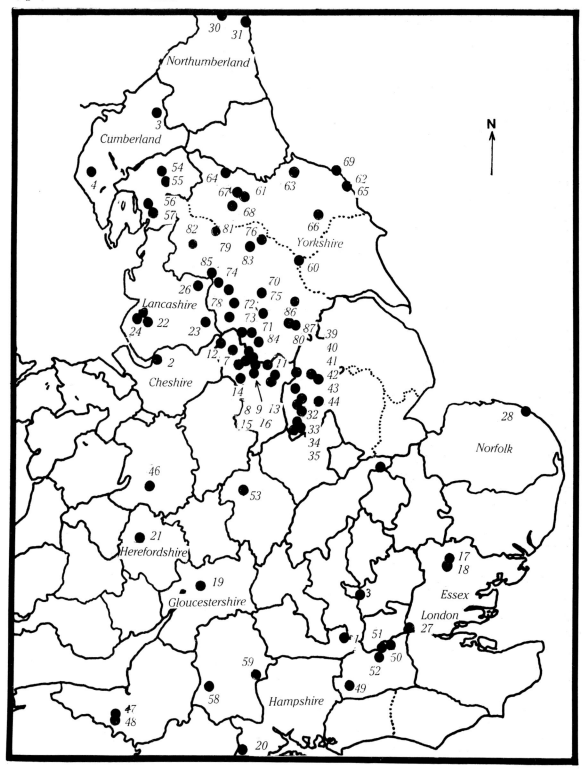

(fig. 5) Robin Hood Place Names
A selective list. County boundaries, pre-April 1974.

Map Reference	O.S. Reference
Berkshire	
1 Robin Hood's Arbour, (Maidenhead)	SU 852811
Cheshire	
2 Robin Hood Butts, (Runcorn)	SJ 488756
Cumberland	
3 Robin Hood Butts, (Farlam)	NY 555587
4 Robin Hood's Chair (Ennerdale Water)	NY 101151
Derbyshire	
5 Robin Hood (near Chesterfield)	SK 278721
6 Robin Hood's Cave (Hathersage)	SK 244836
7 Robin Hood's Chair (Hope Dale)	SK 213820
8 Robin Hood's Croft (near Hathersage)	SK 197867
9 Robin Hood's Cross (near Hathersage)	SK 183802
10 Robin Hood's Leap (Chatsworth)	SK 260690
11 Robin Hood's Moss (overlooking Derwent Dams)	SK 260690
12 Robin Hood's Picking Rods (Glossop)	SK 008909
13 Robin Hood Stoop (Hathersage)	SK 217805
14 Robin Hood's Stride (Bakewell)	SK 223623
15 Robin Hood's Table (near Chesterfield)	SK 277755
16 Robin Hood's Well (near Hathersage)	SK 267799
Essex	
17 Robin Hood End (Finchingfield)	TL 708366
18 Robin Hood End Farm (Finchingfield)	TL 710369
Gloucestershire	
19 Robin's Wood Hill (Gloucester)	SO 841151
Hampshire	
20 Robin Hood's Barrow (Bournemouth)	SZ 070931
Herefordshire	
21 Robin Hood's Butts (Weobley)	SO 430515
Lancashire	
22 Robin Hood (Wrightington, near Wigan)	SD 521115
23 Robin Hood's Bed (near Rochdale)	SD 975165
24 Robin Hood's Field (Scarisbrick)	
25 Robin Hood's Cross (Mawdesley)	SD 519141
26 Robin Hood's House (Burnley)	SD 920346
London	
27 At least eight names in London, some dating from the seventeenth century.	

Norfolk	
28 Robin Friend (Sheringham)	TG 145435
Northamptonshire	
29 Robin Hood and Little John (Peterborough)	TL 140984
Northumberland	
30 Robin Hood's Bog (Chillingham)	NU 079261
31 Robin Hood's Rock (Dunstanburgh)	NU 236273
Nottingham	
32 Three had been recorded by the end of the seventeenth century.	
33 Robin Hood's Acre by 1624/25	
34 Robin Hood's Close by 1485	
35 Robin Hood's Well by 1500	
Nottinghamshire, none can be traced before 1700.	
36 Robin Hood's Cave (Ollerton)	SK 665707
37 Robin Hood's Cave (Mansfield)	SK 510545
38 Robin Hood Farm (near Nottingham)	SK 581494
39 Robin Hood's Grave (Holbeck)	SK 540730
40 Robin Hood Hill (Oxton)	SK 633534
41 Robin Hood's Hill (Mansfield)	SK 515547
42 Robin Hood's Larder (Ollerton)	SK 602675
43 Robin Hood's Meadow (Ollerton)	SK 645709
44 Robin Hood's Stable (near Nottingham)	SK 497492
45 Robin Hood's Well (near Nottingham)	SK 497492
Shropshire	
46 Robin Hood's Butts (Church Stretton)	SO 431966
Somerset	
47 Robin Hood's Butts (Taunton)	ST 230144
48 Robin Hood's Butts (Taunton)	ST 237128
Surrey	
49 Robin Hood's Butts (Godalming)	SU 970478
50 Three names in and around Richmond Park	TQ 205725
51 Robin Hood (Kingston-upon-Thames)	TQ 220720
52 Robin Hood Way	TQ 218700
Warwickshire	
53 Robin Hood's Farm (Birmingham)	SP 110705
Westmoreland	
54 Robin Hood (near Shap)	NY 528060
55 Robin Hood's Grave (Crosby Ravensworth)	NY 617106
56 Robin Hood Island (Kendal)	SD 490885
57 Robin Hood's Wood (Kendal)	SD 490885
Wiltshire	
58 Robin Hood Ball (Netheravon)	SU 144474
59 Robin Hood Bower (Warminster)	ST 876424

York
60 Robin Hood Tower SE 60252

Yorkshire N.
61 Robin Hood (Catterick Bridge) NZ 224004
62 Robin Hood's Bay NZ 952055
63 Robin Hood's Butts (Danby) NZ 712114
64 Robin Hood's Butts
(Barnard Castle) NY 975220
65 Robin Hood's Butts
(Robin Hood's Bay) NZ 963018
66 Robin Hood's Howl (Kirbymoorside) SE 682869
67 Robin Hood's Tower
(Richmond Castle) NZ 172007
68 Robin Hood's Well (Worsley) SE 057866
69 Robin Hood's Close (Whitby) NZ 918096

Yorkshire W.R.
70 Robin Hood (Leeds) SE 326274
71 Robin Hood's Bower and Moss
(Sheffield) SK 355945

72 Robin Hood's Grave (Kirklees) SE 174215
73 Robin Hood's Cottage (Kirklees) SE 173215
74 Robin Hood Hill and House
(Huddersfield) SE 139135
75 Robin Hood Hill (Wakefield) SE 320237
76 Robin Hood's Park (Ripon) SE 260690
77 Robin Hood's Penny Store
(Halifax) SE 018284
78 Robin Hood's Penny Store (Halifax) SE 058248
79 Robin Hood's Store (Skipton) SE 045465
80 Robin Hood's Well (Doncaster) SE 518120
81 Robin Hood's Well (Threshfield) SD 976657
82 Robin Hood's Well (Halton Gill) SD 869786
83 Robin Hood's Well and Wood
(Fountains Abbey) SE 276683
84 Robin Hood's Well (Sheffield) SK 334965
85 Robin Hood Well (Haworth) SE 010370
86 Robin Hood's Stone Skelbrooke
by 1422 SE 505135
87 Robin Hood's Well (A1) SE 519118

When was the age of Robin Hood? 1

In looking at the date of the Robin Hood ballads we have already begun to answer this question. The *Gest*, the longest and one of the earliest of all the ballads, had been constructed out of three separate stories by about 1400. These three stories, and the various tales which each incorporates, must have been circulating in the fourteenth century, if not earlier still. This is indirectly confirmed, of course, by the reference in the poem of *Piers Plowman* of about 1377 to 'rymes of Robyn Hood', which reveals the popularity of some of the ballads – probably but not certainly those found in the *Gest* – in the mid fourteenth century.

The three earliest references to Robin Hood which treat him as a historical character also place him well before 1400; indeed all three place him in a thirteenth century context. John Major in 1521 claimed that Robin Hood was active in the early 1190's (in the reign of Richard I) and would therefore have survived (according to the ballads) well into the thirteenth century. Eighty years earlier, Walter Bower had written that in 1266 'arose the most famous murderer Robert Hood, as well as Little John, together with their accomplices'. Still earlier, and roughly contemporary with the first recorded proverbs mentioning Robin Hood, Andrew of Wyntoun (c. 1420) placed the exploits of Robin and Little John between 1283 and 1285. We do not know on what grounds these dates were suggested, but it seems significant that whilst they all differ, they all agree that Robin Hood was alive in the thirteenth century.

When was the age of Robin Hood?: 2

There is one further source of evidence which throws a little light on the probable period of Robin Hood's activities, or at least the period in which the ballads were first 'composed', and that is the *Gest*. Within this early composite ballad there are six or seven clues.

The most obvious is found at the end of the sixth part (or 'fytte') of the ballad, shortly before the king comes to Nottingham. In stanza 353 the king is referred to by name – Edward. Taken at face value, this would place the story in the period 1272-1307 (the reign of Edward I), if the evidence for a thirteenth century Robin Hood is accepted, or possibly between 1272-1377 (the reigns of Edward I, II and III), if a fourteenth century date is still thought possible. There are two problems to using this clue. The obvious one is that the reference to 'Edwarde, our comely king' may have been inserted into the ballad as a declaration of loyalty to the reigning monarch at the time when the ballad was being composed in the form in which it survives here. The other possibility is that Edward is named as the king who comes to Nottingham and to Sherwood because of all the kings of England, those who paid most recorded visits to Sherwood were, as it happens, Edward I, II and III. (They paid, respectively, five, six and nine visits each). This clue, therefore, though potentially valuable, is not enough evidence on its own.

In a sense, the more reliable clues are those which were unconsciously included in the ballad by its 'composer'. There are perhaps six of these, and the first is a negative one. None of the early ballads, including the *Gest*, make any reference to Justices of the Peace being involved in maintaining the king's authority. From the early fourteenth century Justices were important in this respect, thus their complete absence from the ballads might place their composition before the end of the thirteenth century.

The second clue comes at the very beginning of the *Gest*, in the story of the impoverished knight. In stanza 45 Robin suggests the knight "warte made a knyght of force". The practice of forcing a man to take a knighthood was at its commonest in the reigns of Henry III and Edward I (between 1216 and 1307). This same story provides another clue shortly after (in stanza 55), for at this point the knight declares that he owes the Abbot of St Mary's at York the sum of £400. In the Middle Ages that was a very large sum indeed, and it is generally agreed that by the end of the thirteenth century there were few monasteries which were wealthy enough to advance sums of this size.

Two further clues concern the important role of the Sheriff of Nottingham in the tales of Robin Hood. Next to Robin himself, the Sheriff is the main character, not only in the *Gest*, but in most of the early ballads. He is portrayed as the arch enemy, an evil and corrupt man, and it has been argued that such a portrayal places the composition of the ballads in the period of the Sheriff's greatest powers and unpopularity – before the reign of Edward I began, in 1272. Furthermore, the role of the Sheriff of Nottingham in controlling the forest is one which in real life was rarely given to a sheriff after the middle of the thirteenth century, so that the portrayal of the sheriff in the ballads suggests stories which go back into the earlier thirteenth or late twelfth century.

Again, however, there is a problem in using this evidence. Some scholars believe that the tales of the Sheriff of Nottingham began in a quite separate group of stories which were only incorporated with the ballads of Robin Hood in the later Middle Ages. If that is so, (and no one knows), then of course the pointer to an early thirteenth century date would not necessarily apply to Robin Hood. Clearly, we cannot firmly place an historical Robin Hood with the reigns of any one of Richard I, John, Henry III, and Edward I but it is very unlikely he was active in any later period. If anything, the evidence favours the reign of Henry III (1216-72), bearing in mind the likelihood that the earliest forms of the ballads cannot have been much later than about 1300.

(fig. 6) The Medieval Greenwood
It has been estimated that as early as 1066 only 15% of England was covered with woodland. The woodland that remained in the thirteenth century was intensively managed and provided building timber, wood for tools, furniture and fuel. Such woodland that remained was *therefore jealously guarded and frequently bounded by substantial earthworks. It would be a fortunate outlaw who operated in a district with a large tract of greenwood to serve as a refuge.*

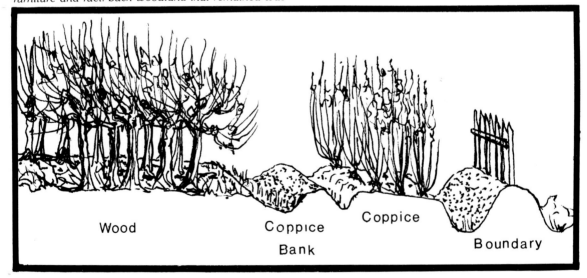

Wood   Coppice   Coppice

Bank   Boundary

WHO WAS THE REAL ROBIN HOOD?

Robin Hood and Sherwood: The Legend

One of the earliest surviving references to Robin Hood, scribbled on a manuscript of the early fifteenth century, reads "Robyn Hod in Scherewod stod" (Robin Hood in Sherwood stood), and that is a truth which any schoolchild will assert. What better place for an outlaw who hunted the king's deer and wore Lincoln Green, than one of the best and most famous of all Royal forests in the kingdom. Here stands the Major Oak where Robin and his men used to gather seven centuries ago; here too until recently stood the hollow tree known as Robin Hood's larder, in which, tradition has it, the outlaws used to hang their venison. Close by are Fountain Dale, believed to be the home of Friar Tuck, and Edwinstowe, where Robin and Maid Marian were married. Around the edges of the Forest are Robin Hood's Cave, Robin Hood's Hill, Robin Hood's Meadow, Robin Hood's Stable, and other places bearing his name. Furthermore, it was in the Forest close to Nottingham that Robin is said to have met the king, who was disguised as a monk (described in the *Gest*), and all the kings possibly associated with Robin Hood, from Richard I to Edward II, are known to have hunted in Sherwood.

Unfortunately, almost all of these associations between Robin Hood and Sherwood are in fact very recent indeed. Major Oak and Robin Hood's Larder were not even saplings in the thirteenth century, Maid Marian does not appear in the Robin Hood story until after the Middle Ages, and none of the place names mentioned above can be traced back beyond the eighteenth century. Is Robin Hood's connection with Sherwood nothing more than myth and legend?

Robin Hood and Sherwood: The Historical Facts

There are two references to Robin Hood in Sherwood in the early ballads. On their own, despite the attractions of Sherwood as a setting for Robin Hood, they would not add up to much. But beyond these two mentions of Sherwood, there are of course many other references to the forest and the greenwood which are closely related to events set in and around Nottingham.

Next to Robin Hood, the most prominent character in the early ballads of Robin Hood is the Sheriff of Nottingham. Nottingham and the Sheriff appear in all three of the earliest surviving ballads. In the *Gest*, Little John is employed in Nottingham by the Sheriff, it is there that the archery contest is held, and there that the king comes to seek and capture Robin Hood. In *Robin Hood and the Monk*, it is to Nottingham that Robin goes, and it is there that he is captured and eventually rescued by Little John and his men. The story of *Robin Hood and the Potter* begins in Yorkshire, but it is to Nottingham that Robin takes his pots, and it is to the Sheriff's wife that he sells them!

In all of these stories, the forest eventually figures, and when the Sheriff and the potter (Robin in disguise) ride into the forest from Nottingham, or when the outlaws escape after the archery competition and seek refuge at Sir Richard of the Lee's castle in the nearby forest, there is really little doubt that the Forest of Sherwood is the forest in question.

Robin Hood's connection with Sherwood may come about by reason of his connection with the Sheriff of Nottingham – his arch enemy – but unless one dispenses with the Sheriff, then Sherwood must remain central to the story of Robin Hood.

Robin Hood and Barnsdale: 1

Despite Sherwood's traditional claim to be the 'home' of Robin Hood, there is no doubt that the

(fig. 7) Sherwood Forest
The aims of the forest laws were to protect the green fodder and deer over large areas which, inevitably, were only partly wooded. Sherwood forest was extended in 1232 and the map shows some of the villages and buildings which stood within the area by the mid thirteenth century.

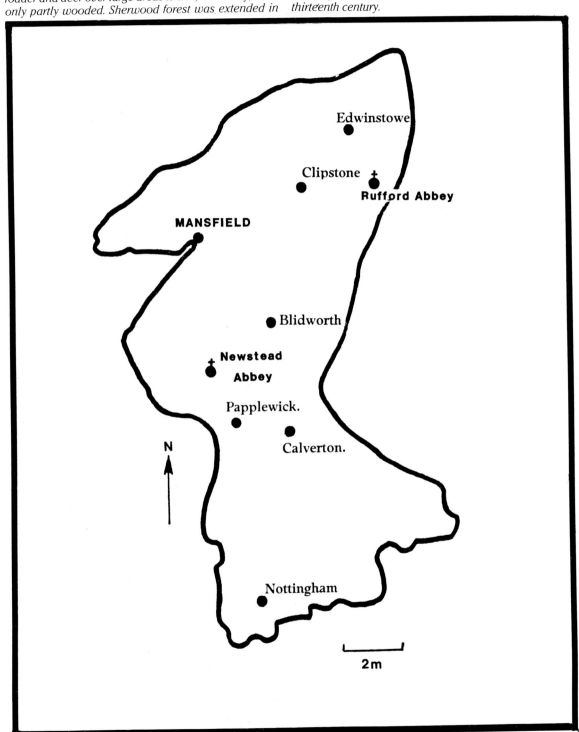

(fig. 8) Barnsdale

The earliest recorded stories of Robin Hood clearly place him in the area of Barnsdale which seems to have included an expanse of open heathland astride the Great North Road. Wentbridge and Saylis also appear in the stories of 'Robin Hood and the Potter' and the 'Gest' respectively. Wentbridge did not stand on the line of the main road in the twelfth century, but the construction of a bridge at Ferrybridge to the north caused a re-alignment of the road through the hamlet in the thirteenth century. By the end of the thirteenth century Wentbridge had become an important stopping place for travellers.

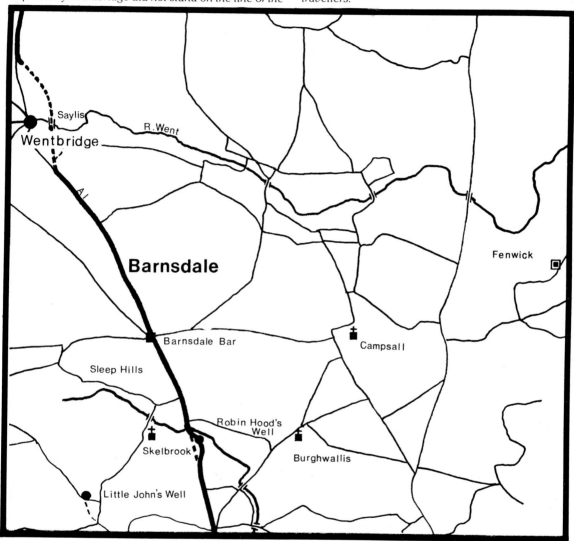

Key

☩	Church
⌇	Road
◙	Moat
●	Well

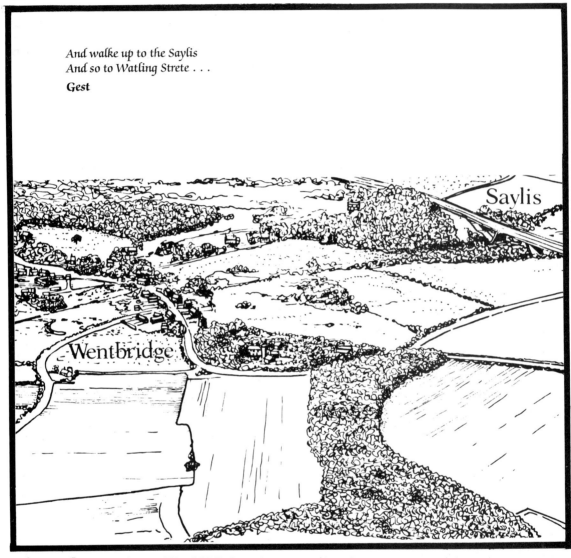

And walke up to the Saylis
And so to Watling Strete . . .
Gest

evidence of the earliest surviving ballads points very clearly to another locale as his original area of activity. Of the five earliest ballads only the story of *Robin Hood and the Monk* is focused on Nottingham. In the ballad of *Robin Hood and Guy of Gisbourne*, Robin identifies himself in no uncertain terms to his opponent – "My name is Robin Hood of Barnsdale", and even before Robin meets Guy, Little John has already returned to Barnsdale, where the rest of Robin's band have been ambushed. The story of *Robin Hood and the Potter* is more specific, for it begins with Little John meeting the potter at 'Wentbreg' – the village of Wentbridge, where the Great North Road crosses the river Went.

The *Gest* is more specific still, for at the outset of the story Robin tells Little John to "walke up to the Saylis and so to Watlinge Strete". Saylis (or Sayles) was a small tenancy of the manor of Pontefract, and is situated just over a quarter of a mile to the east of Wentbridge, commanding a view along the Great North Road – which at this point was known in the thirteenth century as Watling Street! There is no doubt at all that the meeting with the impoverished knight on his way to York took place here, a dozen miles north of Doncaster.

Finally, the ballad of *The Death of Robin Hood* has Robin journeying to the priory at Kirklees, only 15 miles from Barnsdale, where he eventually meets his end at the hands of the prioress and Sir Roger of Doncaster.

Robin Hood and Barnsdale: 2

The dominant role of Barnsdale and surrounding places – often very localised places – in its vicinity in the early ballads leaves little room for doubt that Robin Hood's activities were placed here by the minstrels and balladeers of the fourteenth century. This association of Robin with Barnsdale is found at an early date outside the ballads too. The earliest of the historical chroniclers to refer to Robin Hood, Andrew of Wyntoun, (c. 1420), refers to Robin

Hood and Little John as being active in "Ingilwode and Bernysdaile". The reference to Inglewood in Cumbria suggests a certain confusion with some other lengendary outlaws of this period, in particular Adam Bell and his associates, but this does not diminish the significance of the reference to Barnsdale, nor the omission of Sherwood. Only a few years later in 1429, we find a legal formula in a lawsuit repeating the information – "Robin Hode in Barnsdale strode". Thus the ballads and the few other early records which refer to Robin's whereabouts come down very firmly in favour of Barnsdale and the area immediately around it as his original scene of action. One would give a great deal to find a copy of a now lost ballad which was paraphrased in 1440 by Robert Bower, and which told the story of how a certain Sheriff was outwitted in Barnsdale, for this ballad might help to unravel the mystery of Barnsdale and Sherwood in the story of Robin Hood.

(fig. 10) The supposed grave of Robin Hood

Sherwood and Barnsdale

There is clearly a contradiction between the early ballads and popular tradition, as to where the main focus of Robin Hood's activity lay. The contradiction occurs, however, even within the ballads, for Robin's persistent enemy there is the Sheriff of Nottingham, who would have no jurisdiction over matters in Barnsdale. Various attempts have been made to explain the mystery. Some have argued that the Barnsdale of the *Gest* is really Bryunsdale, near Basford on the edge of Nottingham. But such a solution does not explain the very precise references to Sayles, Wentbridge, Watling Street, and Kirklees – which all belong very firmly in and around the Yorkshire Barnsdale. A more likely solution is that there were originally two quite separate sets of stories – one about Robin Hood and one about the Sheriff of Nottingham – and these became linked, and then eventually interwoven. This is the solution favoured by several leading scholars who have studied the ballads. There remains, however, at least the possibility that Robin Hood in Barnsdale is not incompatible with Robin Hood in Sherwood. First, contemporary court records show that in the Middle Ages, the activities of any one outlaw band could range over several counties. Second, the northern tip of Sherwood is only 30 miles from Barnsdale, and rapid movement from one to the other is recorded in many instances, some of which are particularly interesting. In 1194, for example, Richard I chased a deer all the way from Sherwood Forest to Barnsdale! In 1213 King John travelled from Rothwell, just north of Barnsdale, to Nottingham, in the space of a single day. In 1275 several of a group of armed men who had rescued two deer poachers apprehended in Sherwood Forest fled to Yorkshire when pursued. Clearly, it was possible for those hunting deer and those fleeing the law to move easily from Sherwood to Barnsdale and beyond, and Robin Hood could have been active in both areas. Since the earliest ballads lay such heavy emphasis on Barnsdale, it seems likely that this was his original scene of activity, but it is possible that as his band grew in numbers so he moved to Sherwood where it was much easier to hide in safety than in the very restricted woodland of Barnsdale.

It is now possible to locate Robin Hood very firmly in the area of Barnsdale to the north of Doncaster, but it should be recognised that he could also have been active in north Nottinghamshire, and we have suggested that he lived in the thirteenth century. Can we find any historical references to a Robin Hood during this period and in these areas? Surprisingly the answer is yes, but before we look at these we should perhaps exclude from consideration some of the other Robin Hoods who have sometimes been identified as our legendary hero.

One of them is, at first sight, a particularly attractive candidate – the Robin Hood who is recorded as being imprisoned in 1354 for no less a crime than trespass of 'vert and venison' in a royal forest. But the Forest is that of Rockingham, in Northamptonshire, an area with which the legendary Robin Hood has had no connections, and the period is really too late to be seriously considered.

A much earlier Robin Hood, who would fit neatly into the traditional picture of activity in the reign of Richard I and King John, is recorded as having slain Ralph of Cirencester around 1213-1216. Certainly an offence which might have made Robin an outlaw, but this Robin was a servant of the Abbot of Cirencester, and the event took place there, a very long way indeed from Barnsdale.

Finally, we should perhaps consider the case of the follower of Simon de Montfort who, after de Montfort's defeat at the Battle of Evesham in 1265 became an outlaw in Sherwood. Henry III offered 100 marks to the Constable of Nottingham Castle to capture him, so that here we have a Sherwood outlaw, pursued by the Constable of Nottingham, in the very period to which the legendary Robin would seem to belong. Unfortunately, this outlaw is recorded under the name Roger Godberd, and there is no reason to think he was ever known by any other name.

There remain two figures who occur in historical records who might possibly have been the original Robin Hood.

We know most about a Robert Hood of Wakefield, less than ten miles west of Barnsdale. This Robert Hood appears on a number of occasions in the Court Rolls for Wakefield – that is, in the records of the activities of the Wakefield court – during the period 1308-1315. He was charged with, and found guilty of, taking firewood from both the Outwood and the Old and New Parks of Wakefield. As a result he was reprimanded and fined on a number of occasions.

He may well be the same Robin Hood who is recorded as buying a plot of land on Bickhill (the market place of Wakefield) in 1316, and in this year we find his wife's name recorded too. Her name was Matilda, and as chance would have it, later tradition said that Maid Marian's name was originally Matilda. This is unlikely, however, for the whole story of Robin and Maid Marian is a post medieval development. Maid Marian appears in none of the original ballads.

So far then, our Robin Hood lives near Barnsdale and is a persistent if minor offender against the law. In 1332 came events which might have turned him into an outlaw. King Edward's army met and conquered the army of the Earl of Lancaster at Boroughbridge. Robin Hood of Wakefield would have owed his allegiance to the Earl and if he was amongst the defeated troops at Boroughbridge may well have fled to the forest and lived the life of an outlaw. The subsequent visit of Edward to Yorkshire, Lancashire and Nottingham in 1323 might then be reflected in the King's appearance in these areas in the *Gest*. According to the *Gest* it was during a visitation by King Edward that Robin was pardoned and taken into the king's service. Amazingly, the records of Edward's household from June 1323 to November 1324 mention amongst Edward's valets, one 'Robyn Hod', who eventually (like the Robin Hood of the *Gest*) leaves the king's service. According to the *Gest* Robin then returned to Barnsdale and took up his old way of life, and in 1329 sure enough, we find a record of a robbery at the Sayles — Robin's old haunt — committed by "two men of Doncaster and others". Here, clearly, we have a very plausible historical Robin Hood, whose story fits remarkably closely to that of the legendary hero. Or does it?

At first glance Robert Hood of Wakefield looks very much like the Robin Hood of the ballads, but the similarity is largely illusion. All we know of Robin Hood of Wakefield is that he lived in the early fourteenth century near Barnsdale and committed minor offences for which he paid minor fines. We do not know if he was at Boroughbridge, nor if he ever became an outlaw, and certainly we do not know if he had any connection at all with the

'Robyn Hod' in Edward's household or with the robbery at the Sayles in 1329. Historically, it is extremely unlikely that Edward would have welcomed one of Lancaster's common soldiers into his household within twelve months of Boroughbridge. It is even more unlikely that a Robin Hood who became an outlaw in 1322 and joined the king's household in 1323 would have made such an impact on the popular imagination in the early fourteenth century.

Of our remaining candidates for the legendary hero we have another Robert Hood of West Yorkshire who appears in a Pipe Roll (record of payments to the exchequer) of 1226. Although we know little of this man, the one piece of information we are given is significant, for this Robert Hood is described as a fugitive, and the Roll refers to penalties of 32s.6d. for his chattels. A marginal note for a subsequent year, when the account recurred indicates that this Robert Hood was a tenant of the Archbishop of York. The nearest of the Archbishop's tenancies to Barnsdale lay in the villages north of Ferrybridge, only five miles north of Wentbridge. Obviously on such flimsy information we cannot firmly identify this man as the original Robin Hood — all we can say is that we have a Robert Hood living in the right place at the right time, and that this man (for reasons unknown) was a fugitive around 1226.

What certainly does emerge from the Yorkshire records is that around Barnsdale and Wakefield in the thirteenth and early fourteenth centuries there were several, possibly related, Hood families. At least seven of their menfolk in this period carried the name Robert (or Robyn). Unfortunately, the earliest surviving Court Rolls for Wakefield go back only to 1274 — otherwise we might have learned more about the 'fugitive' of 1226. It does seem likely, however, that it is amongst the Hoods of the Wakefield district that we should look for the real Robin Hood! A further piece of evidence which strengthens the case for the thirteenth century candidates is a discovery in the Memoranda Roll of 1262, (Henry III). In the Roll the clerk had changed the name of one William son of Robert the Smith to William Robehod. William was a fugitive whose goods had been siezed by the prior of Sandleford. It appears that at some point a clerk associated the activities of William with Robin Hood's and described him thus. This suggests that as early as 1262 our subject's name was used to describe a fugitive from justice.

ROBIN HOOD CHARACTERS

The Sheriff of Nottingham

Next to Robin himself, the Sheriff of Nottingham is the most prominent character in the early ballads of Robin Hood. From the very beginning of the *Gest* where Robin warns Little John to beware of the Sheriff of Nottingham he is Robin's principal opponent, and a man to be hated and feared. The hostility displayed towards the Sheriff in the ballads should come as no surprise. For two hundred years the Sheriffs had been enforcing oppressive measures against the common people and extortion and corruption were commonly associated with them. What is surprising, however, is that in the early ballads, set, as we have seen, in the vicinity of Barnsdale, it is the Sheriff of Nottingham who figures so prominently. The apparent contradiction is so great that many scholars believe there must originally have been two quite separate sets of stories – one about Robin Hood and one about the Sheriff of Nottingham and they later became interwoven. But it is difficult to explain how they became so closely intertwined, and certainly there are no surviving fragments of an early set of ballads about the Sheriff of Nottingham alone. One possible explanation, is that Robin Hood was active both in Barnsdale and Sherwood, either moving from one to the other as necessity and opportunity determined, or perhaps beginning his career in Barnsdale and later moving his activities 30-40 miles further south.

If we accept that there may have been a Sheriff of Nottingham who was indeed the implacable enemy of Robin Hood, then any attempt to identify him in the historical records must be preceded by a brief consideration of the office he would have held. First it must be made clear that our man would not have been 'The Sheriff of Nottingham' – this title and office was not created until 1449, certainly too late for Robin's Sheriff. In the thirteenth and fourteenth centuries there were in fact four officers who might have been the prototype of Robin's enemy. First

there was the Sheriff of Nottinghamshire and Derbyshire, second there was the Sheriff of Yorkshire. Thirdly, there was the Constable of Nottingham Castle, and fourthly there were the Chief Justices of the Forest.

Amongst early fourteenth century candidates for the role of Robin's foe were John de Oxenford and Sir Robert Ingram, Sheriffs of Nottinghamshire and Derbyshire in 1334-39 and 1328-33 respectively. Oxenford was known to have been corrupt and unpopular. Furthermore, since during his period as Sheriff the Exchequer sat at York, he would have had to travel through Barnsdale to present his accounts! Ingram was equally corrupt and actually aided a gang of outlaws in North Derbyshire.

A third fourteenth century candidate is John, Baron de Segrave, who was a very unpopular Justice of the Forests beyond the Trent (1308-15) and Keeper of Nottingham Castle (1308-25).

A fourth (fourteenth century candidate) is Sir Henry de Faucumberg who was at various times between 1318 and 1330 Sheriff of Nottingham-shire and Derbyshire, Sheriff of Yorkshire, as well as being Constable of Nottingham Castle in 1325.

Faucumberg had possible connections with a fourteenth century Robin Hood. A Henry Fauconberg is mentioned on five occasions in the Wakefield Manor Court Rolls between 1313 and 1315 and in 1328 (as the name was so rare it was likely to have been the same person in spite of the spelling difference). Did he first here come into conflict with the fourteenth century Robert Hood of Wakefield? If so possibly the enmity worsened after the Earl of Lancaster's defeat in 1322 when our Robert Hood of Wakefield may have been on the Earl's side and Fauconberg is assumed to have been on the side of the King.

Faucumberg is also known to have been unpopular, with complaints of extortions and false imprisonment being made against him. He also took part in attempts to track down the notorious bandit Eustace de Folville and his associate Ralph le Zouche.

The offices held by both de Segrave and Faucumberg gave both of them scope to come into contact with a fourteenth century Robin Hood. Even if one does not accept the idea of the fourteenth century Robin Hood both could still be the Sheriff of the *Gest* and they may have helped to focus some of the ballads of Robin Hood on Nottingham.

(fig. 11) The Sheriff
The sheriff was the king's representative in the county and he sought to administer justice. He enforced the law, *gathered taxes and dues, generally travelling the countryside with an armed escort.*

In the thirteenth century there are three more candidates for the original Sheriff of Nottingham. Philip Mark was Sheriff of Nottinghamshire and Derbyshire 1209-1224 and as custodian of Sherwood too in the period 1212-17 he may have come into conflict with the outlaw. A more promising candidate perhaps is Brian de Lisle who was chief forester of Nottinghamshire and Derbyshire 1209-17, Chief Justice of the Forest 1221-1224, and Sheriff of Yorkshire 1233-34. His activities both in the royal forests of Nottinghamshire and as Sheriff of Yorkshire might be the background for Robin's Sheriff.

There remains the third candidate, and he is perhaps the most plausible of all. Eustace of Loudham was Sheriff of Yorkshire in 1225-26, Forest Justice north of the Trent 1232-33, and Sheriff of Nottinghamshire and Derbyshire 1232-33. Here is a man who was Sheriff with jurisdiction over both Barnsdale and Nottingham, who also administered the royal forests. If he were the original 'Sheriff of Nottingham' it is relatively easy to understand how he came to be involved with tales revolving around Barnsdale. There is one further point in his favour too. It was Eustace of Loudham who, as Sheriff of Yorkshire, would have been responsible for collecting and accounting for the penalties imposed on Robert Hode – fugitive, in 1226. It is possible – no more – that here we have the crucial clue to the historical identity of both Robin and the Sheriff, and an explanation of Robin Hood's vehement hatred of the man.

Little John

Little John is Robin's right-hand man and faithful companion. He appears in stanza 3 of the *Gest*, is found in all the early ballads, and is there at the end in the ballad of *The Death of Robin Hood*.

It is possible that 'Little John' was no more than an alias, in which case a search of historical records for the historical John would be pointless. One tradition has it that his name was originally John Little, whilst in the ballad of *Little John and the Sheriff*, John himself tells the Sheriff 'they call me Reynold Greenleaf when I am at home', and says he was born in Holderness, which also happens to be the birthplace of Sir Henry de Faucumberg.

Documentary evidence produces several possible candidates for Little John. There is a reference in the Court Rolls of Wakefield to Little John de Cockroft of Sowerby in 1324. Also a 'Little John' is

recorded as breaking into the Archbishop of York's park at Beverley in Yorkshire in 1323 and stealing his deer. This is the usual crime associated with Robin Hood's band, and typically a leading churchman is the victim. Moreover Beverley is quite close to Holderness. These fourteenth century candidates may possibly be the same person as 'Little John' who is mentioned in the king's household records (1322-1325). He served the king as a sailor and commanded a Royal ship in January 1325, transporting the king's goods from Nottingham to London. While it may seem unusual that Little John was a sailor this evidence would link him with Robyn Hood who left the King's service in 1325 and furthermore may place him as the Little John of the *Gest*.

(fig. 12) Little John's Grave Slab
The grave slab now resting in the porch of Hathersage church bears the initials L.I. The cross on the slab is carved in a style current in the late thirteenth century whilst the letters seem to have been carved into the stone at a later date.

The only thirteenth century candidate is from an entry in the Wakefield Rolls which refers to Robert Little. Apart from the surname there is no other evidence to connect him to the famous outlaw.

The only other quasi-historical testimony to a real Little John comes from the Derbyshire village of Hathersage. Here, there still survives a medieval **grave-slab with the initials L.I. carved upon it.** The stone stood at the head of a grave, traditionally that of Little John, which was opened in 1784 and contained amongst other things a massive thigh-bone. In the adjacent church, his bow, quiver and arrows were said to have hung until removed in 1729. The bow, some 79 in. (about 2m.) long, was kept in Cannon Hall, Barnsley, until 1951 and was first recorded in the church in 1652. How long it had hung there we do not know, but Little John's association with Hathersage clearly goes back at least several centuries and it is possible that if he was more than a figment of the balladeer's imagination, then he did indeed end his days here, some 30 miles from both Barnsdale and Sherwood.

The Merry Men

Just as the name Little John might be an alias, so might those of other of the 'merry men' in the Robin Hood legend. Nevertheless, it is interesting to look briefly at these characters both in the ballads and in historical documents.

Much the Miller's son and Will Scarlet both appear in the *Gest* as early as stanza 4. They accompany Little John to find a guest for dinner and meet the knight. Much the Miller also appears in the story *Robin Hood and the Monk*. History throws no light on him, but we do know that there were at least three windmills in the vicinity of Wakefield around 1270, and another is recorded near Wentbridge in 1313. There were in fact many mills in West Yorkshire in the Middle Ages, and in the east of the county – which seems to be Robin Hood country – these were mainly windmills, due to a lack of sufficient water power for mills. Will Scarlett also appears in the other early ballads (*Robin Hood and the Monk, Death of Robin Hood*, and *Robin Hood and Guy of Gisbourne*), so that he too may claim to

(fig. 13) The Thirteenth Century Mill
Windmills appeared in England by the end of the twelfth century and by the middle of the following century they were a familiar feature of the landscape. In order to take *advantage of variable winds the post mill was developed.*

(fig. 14) The Thirteenth Century Knight
Knighthood in the thirteenth century was not necessarily a state to be sought in view of the expenses and obligations involved. Many knights were poor and such characters frequently appear in medieval literature.

be an original part of the story. Although he is called Scarlett in the *Death of Robin Hood,*, in the *Gest* he is called Scarlock and Scathelocke, and in *Robin Hood and the Monk* he is Scathlock. This is interesting since this is certainly a real name in use in West Yorkshire in the Middle Ages, recorded in an Assize Roll in 1372 and 1381; a Schakelok is recorded in Wakefield Court Rolls in 1317.

Will Stuteley and Alan-a-Dale, alas, cannot be traced back to the original ballads. Will Stuteley appears in only two ballads, both of seventeenth century date, whilst Alan-a-Dale first appears in a ballad towards the end of the same century.

Sir Richard of the Lee
Sir Richard of the Lee is commonly assumed to be the impoverished knight who appears at the beginning of the *Gest,* although this knight is never mentioned by name. He is entertained to dinner by Robin Hood who learns of the knight's poverty and that he owes money to the Abbot of St. Mary's. Robin then loans the money to the knight. It is thought that the knight came from Wyresdale (in Lancashire) where there is a hamlet called Lee. According to the *Gest* Sir Richard of the Lee, (first named in stanza 310), had a castle near Nottingham where he provided refuge for Robin Hood and his band.

It has been suggested that the prototype for Sir Richard is one Sir Richard Foliot, a knight of Nottinghamshire who owned lands on the edge of Sherwood and associated in the 1270s with the outlaw Roger Godberd who we saw earlier as a possible contender for recognition as the original Robin Hood. Richard Foliot also owned a castle at Fenwick and land at Norton, close to Barnsdale Bar – the haunt of Robin Hood. From the same region there are records in the mid fourteenth century of a Richard de Leigh, and as early as 1317 a Richard of the Lee appears in the Wakefield Court Rolls.

Not only is the knight a central figure in the early part of the *Gest,* but there is also an emphasis on chivalrous and courteous behaviour, leading some to believe that the whole story of the knight was inserted into the *Gest* as a propoganda exercise for the virtues of knighthood.

Sir Guy of Gisbourne
While Sir Richard of the Lee is said to represent the ideal knight, Sir Guy of Gisbourne is the evil villain even more so than the Sheriff in the Robin Hood stories.

However, in the ballad of *Robin Hood and Guy of Gisbourne*, Gisbourne is a yeoman who meets Robin and informs him that he is seeking an outlaw, 'Robin Hood'. After a long struggle Robin slays Guy and then, according to the ballad, 'he took Sir Guy's head by the hair and stuck it on the end of his bow', saying 'you have been a traitor all your life, to which there must come an end'. This act does not appear to be merely one of brutality but seems to have some other significance. It does bear a striking resemblance to the hunting scene in an illustrated 'Book of Hours', written about 1300, where a stag's head is placed onto the end of a pole by a hunter.

(fig. 15) Women's dress in the thirteenth century

27

The story of Guy of Gisbourne and Robin also survives in the form of a play dated to 1475. This would have been performed for village audiences and probably helped to increase the popularity of the story. The play suggests a further symbolic meaning to the story. Robin in green symbolises the triumph of spring over winter which is taken to be Gisbourne dressed in a sterile brown horse hide.

It is assumed that Guy of Gisbourne takes his name from the village of Gisburn which is only ten miles from Wyresdale, which itself is associated with Sir Richard of the Lee. The story may have been a separate tale and made its way into the Robin Hood stories from west of the Pennines.

The Abbot of St Mary's, The Prioress of Kirklees, and Sir Roger of Doncaster

Apart from the Sheriff and Sir Guy, the Abbot, the Prioress and Sir Roger represent the enemies of Robin Hood in the early ballads. The fact that all three appear in the earliest ballads suggests they may indeed have been historical personages, or at least original figures in the story of Robin Hood, or possibly both.

St Mary's certainly seems to have been unpopular with the local people in the mid-thirteenth century. The Abbot is believed to have been over zealous in the rent collecting. In 1262 the people of York slew several monks from the Abbey. It was also well capable of lending large amounts of money, such as that borrowed by the knight in the very first tale in the *Gest*; in 1304 it sent £4,000 to Edward I in Scotland. What little we know of the thirteenth century Abbey then fits well enough with its portrayal in the *Gest* as both wealthy and despised.

If one accepts a fourteenth century Robin Hood there are two possible candidates for the Prioress of Kirklees. Firstly, Alice de Serevon is mentioned in the Wakefield Court Rolls in 1315 and 1331. She is thus a contemporary of Robert Hood of Wakefield. Secondly, Elizabeth de Staynton (her grave slab was discovered in 1706), who some say was related to Robin, is thought to have been Prioress at about the time Robin died according to the *Gest* in 1346/7, two and a half years after he had left the Royal Household.

Thirteenth century prioresses include a Sybil and a Joanna de Stainton. The bad light in which the Priory is shown in the story of Robin's death accords with its poor reputation as on several occasions its nuns were accused of philandering with men.

Finally, there is Sir Roger of Doncaster, who assists the Prioress in killing Robin. Again, the fourteenth century records contain a man of this name, a contemporary of Robert Hood of Wakefield. The Wakefield Court Roll for 1327 mentions one 'Roger, son of William de Doncastre', who is said to be a chaplain. Neither of these men, it should be noted, is a knight but that is not an unsuperable problem if one believes that Robin Hood lived at this time. If we take the view that he lived two generations earlier, the absence of the Court Rolls for Wakefield means we have no historical Sir Rogers to consider.

Maid Marian

In the twentieth century, in films and books, Maid Marian is one of the most important characters in the story of Robin Hood – a royal ward who risks all to live with Robin in the greenwood. Those who identify Robin with the fourteenth century Robert Hood of Wakefield associate Marian with Robert's wife Matilda, otherwise the association between Robin and Marian is uncertain in origin.

One link may be the French play 'Robin and Marian' composed in 1283 which bears some resemblance to the popular romantic story of Robin Hood and Maid Marian. The play was well known throughout Europe, but it is uncertain whether or not it influenced early writers. When the monk Alexander Barclay of Ely said in his work 'Ship of Fools', written in 1500, 'Some merry fit (poem) of Maid Marian or els of Robin Hood', he was in this sentence implying that they were separate individuals. Marian later appears as the outlaw's companion in a seventeenth century Broadsheet Ballad *'Robin Hood and Maid Marian'*. What caused the post medieval writers to link them in romantic love when earlier writers had not? It is possible that the story of Robin and Marian became popular through the Games and May Festivities of the sixteenth century. The May Queen seems to have taken the title Maid Marian and then her companion, the Lord of the May or May King, later took that of Robin Hood.

Friar Tuck

Friar Tuck also played a prominent role in the May

(fig. 16) The Betley Window, 1621 (from Betley Old Hall, Staffordshire)

The character of Robin Hood became associated with May Games. One of the earliest surviving illustrations of such games, at Betley includes a May Queen and a friar, but no Robin Hood.

Festivals, and that may partly explain the reason for his subsequent popularity as a character in the Robin Hood story. However, it has been suggested that Friar Tuck may have been a real person. Robert Stafford, a chaplain of Lindfield in Sussex, assumed the name 'Frere Tuck' when he led an outlaw band in 1417. It is possible that a minor outlaw such as Stafford adopted such a strange name because Friar Tuck was already a well established character in the Robin Hood story. He may also have been acquainted with the Robin Hood story because his parish of Lindfield was adjacent to Fletching where Gilbert Robynhood was recorded in 1292. Gilbert Robynhood does have a strong case for a link to the Robin Hood area of Yorkshire through the House of Lancaster and the Lacys. Alice, the heiress of the Lacy estates was betrothed to Thomas, Earl of Lancaster, heir to the Liberty of Leicester in Sussex, where Gilbert was a tenant.

The problem in tracing Friar Tuck is a lack of documentary evidence. He is not mentioned in the *Gest* but first appears in the 1475 play of *Robin Hood and Guy of Gisborne*. There is also a ballad *Robin Hood and the Curtall Fryer* which is of a later date. This Curtall Fryer appears to be a different character to Friar Tuck. However, there are some general points which may help to link Friar Tuck with a thirteenth century Robin Hood.

Although the Friars did not appear in England until 1221, they were 1200 in number by 1250, and in that year a House of Greyfriars was founded at Broadmarsh near Nottingham Castle, and also near York Castle in 1230 so that a thirteenth century Robin Hood could have met a wayward Friar. The Friars, moreover, were initially regarded as the people's friend, and so were more likely than other members of the clergy to become associated with an outlaw figure such as Robin Hood.

The growth of the Robin Hood Story from the Sixteenth Century

Our search for a historic Robin Hood and his associates has taken us back as far as the thirteenth century in the reign of Henry III. The ballads of Robin Hood as they developed from that time were probably directed at the yeomen of a feudal household such as the Lacys. Robin himself is described as a yeoman as is Guy of Gisbourne. The ballads for this audience, however, bear little resemblance to the present day legend. It seems

that the story has undergone a process of change and adaption over the centuries.

The story came to take on a wider audience at the end of the fifteenth century and during the sixteenth century. It was through the popularity of the plays and games of that time and the incorporation of Robin Hood into the May Festivals that he and Maid Marian, Friar Tuck and Little John became best known. King Henry VIII, (1509-1547) is known to have encouraged the games and indeed enjoyed dressing up as Robin Hood. However, in some areas Robin Hood games served as a form of social protest against the land owning class with Robin being known as 'Lord of Inobedience'. The symbolic palace for the Lord built next to the traditional Maypole was made of boughs by convention taken from the woodlands of the wealthy.

It is interesting to note that these festivities were popular in areas largely outside the historic homeland of Robin Hood, Yorkshire, Derbyshire and Nottinghamshire. It seems that in those counties he was accepted as a real person, and could not easily be adopted as a mythical figure. After the Reformation the Robin Hood plays and other festivities were frowned upon and discouraged, indeed seventeenth century writers speak of the Robin Hood games as a thing of the past. It seemed that only the Maypole had survived. Robin Hood does, however, enter the Shakespearean tradition in 'As you like it' where he becomes part of an idyllic woodland world of the Forest of Arden.

As a figure, Robin had become politically safer by the end of the sixteenth century, having been gentrified in Anthony Munday's 'The Downfall of Robert Earl of Huntingdon', and much of the popular legend stems from this source.

It was during the seventeenth century that the Robin Hood stories reached a wider literary audience by means of broad sheet ballads. In the eighteenth century Joseph Ritson, who made the first comprehensive collection of ballads, emphasised Robin as a social rebel, but it was in the nineteenth century that the final strands were added to the popular legend. The romantic revival of that period saw a renewed interest in the Middle Ages, and it was Walter Scott in 'Ivanhoe' who first introduced the idea of Robin as a Saxon struggling against the Normans. Writers then viewed the accumulation of myth, romance and adventure in the Robin Hood story as suitable material for children. Pierce Egan's 'Robin Hood and Little John', written in 1840, was the first such work, and 'The Merry Adventures of Robin Hood', the work of American author Howard Pyle in 1883 was the basis for future film epics. The twentieth century media has further enhanced the picture of an adventure story with heroes and villains so that the Robin Hood of today has travelled a long distance from a thirteenth century bandit.

Robin Hood has become an indelible part of our culture and folk lore through the numerous place names associated with him and because he has come to be seen as the original people's protector against authority. When plans for a modern housing estate threatened the rural charm of part of the Nottinghamshire Robin Hood country, protest posters were signed . . . Robin Hood.

(fig. 17) Steetley Chapel
The attractive little Norman chapel at Steetley near Worksop, is traditionally linked with Robin Hood. It has been said that Friar Tuck brought Robin and his men for prayers at the chapel. Tradition further asserts that Alan-a-Dale was married here, but both Alan and Friar Tuck are considered to be late additions to the story of Robin Hood.

ROBIN HOOD PLACES

Abbeys and Priories

Next to the Sheriff of Nottingham, wicked churchmen seem to be the most prolific of Robin's enemies – from the Abbot of St Mary's in the first part of the Gest, through the villainous monk in *Robin Hood and the Monk*, to the treacherous Prioress of Kirklees in *The Death of Robin Hood*.

St Mary's Abbey was, in fact, the richest in Yorkshire. It was founded in 1087 by Benedictine monks, but there is little surviving trace of its walls, built of Tadcaster limestone.

The same, alas, is true of Kirklees Priory on the outskirts of Leeds. All that survives is a part of the restored and reconstructed gatehouse of this Cistercian nunnery. Some 650 yards from the gatehouse is the supposed burial of Robin Hood. A famous medieval gravestone was found here and recorded in a gazatteer of 1584. A drawing of the gravestone made in 1665 still survives, but little of the stone remains. The drawing of the gravestone includes a partial inscription which clearly reads: "Here lie Robard Hude, William Goldsburgh, Thomas . . ." Who William and Thomas were we have no idea; it is possible, in view of these names being written down one margin below the arms of the cross carved on the stone, that they were added at a later date and that the stone originally contained the name of Robard Hude alone.

One other monastery in Yorkshire which has sometimes been associated with the story of Robin Hood is Fountains Abbey. The abbey is mentioned by name in the ballad of *Robine Hood and Fryer Tucke* and in *Robin Hood and the Curtall Fryer*. Although both ballads may have had late medieval forerunners, they are both of late date, as indeed is the appearance of Friar Tuck in the story of Robin Hood. Furthermore, if Friar Tuck lived at Fountains Abbey he would not have been a Friar at all, but a Cistercian monk. Nevertheless, a visit to the abbey is to be recommended!

Barnsdale

If you look at a modern map of the area north of Doncaster and Barnsley you will have to look hard to find 'Barnsdale', but it is there, about 8 miles, (12 kms) north-west of Doncaster along the A1 – the Great North Road. There is good reason to believe that this is where the original Robin Hood was active, but if that is so, then our ideas about Robin and the 'Greenwood' have to be modified.

Barnsdale was never legally a 'forest', and medieval records suggest that it was not heavily wooded. Neither was it extensive – in the sixteenth century the name seems to have been used for an area about five miles square south of Ferrybridge. But this small wooded area was nevertheless notorious in the Middle Ages as the lair of robbers who made a living by waylaying travellers on the Great North Road in the vicinity of the junction at Barnsdale Bar. In 1307 when the Bishop of St Andrews journeyed from Scotland to Winchester, the number of archers protecting him was doubled at this point on his journey, specifically "on account of Barnsdale". There is little to see in Barnsdale today that would remind you of Robin Hood's forest, but the village of Wentbridge which figures in the story of Robin Hood and the Potter is still there. Wentbridge was a settlement by at least the end of the twelfth century, and several medieval references to it suggest it was an important stopping place for travellers on the Great North Road. Close by, and overlooking Wentbridge and the Road, just as the *Gest* tells us, is Sayles – today the name of a plantation, but in Robin's day a land-holding in the parish of Kirk Smeaton. This spot's value as a look-out position over the Great North Road is apparent even today.

(fig. 18) St. Mary's Abbey, York

St. Mary's Abbey was one of the most powerful in England and appears early in the 'Gest' when the Abbot demanded repayment of a debt by mortgage from a poor knight. Had the knight failed to pay, the Abbot would have gained further land for St. Mary's and if the event was set after 1279 it would have been illegal. Strictly speaking monastic houses were prevented from expanding their landed estates by the 'Statute of Mortmain' (1279) unless they had a Royal license. Furthermore in the 1270's St. Mary's embarked upon a huge rebuilding programme and would not, presumably, have been in a position to take up a mortgage of any size. St. Mary's was unpopular and in 1262 the people of York had caused the Abbot to flee after burning some of his buildings and killing a number of his tenants. Soon after these events the Abbey precincts were protected by a stone wall.

The reconstruction shows the Abbey as it may have appeared in the middle of the thirteenth century before the great rebuilding.

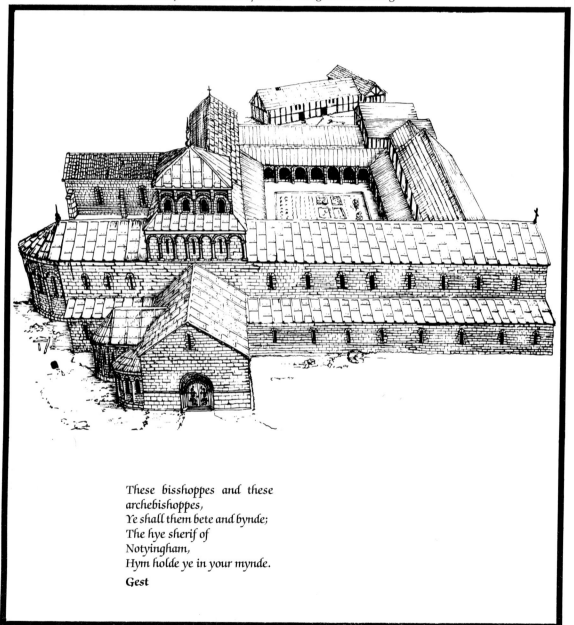

These bisshoppes and these
archebishoppes,
Ye shall them bete and bynde;
The hye sherif of
Notyingham,
Hym holde ye in your mynde.

Gest

33

(fig. 19) Kirklees Priory
Little is known about the original appearance of the Cistercian nunnery of Kirklees save for an etching of the gatehouse printed in 1795. The reconstruction shows a Cistercian nun standing before the gatehouse.

A little over three miles south of Sayles and Wentbridge by the side of the A1 stands Robin Hood's well, a famous halting place already in the seventeenth century, where passengers stopped to drink the water. In the eighteenth century Lord Carlisle employed Vanburgh to build a stone archway over the site. How much older the name is we do not know, but not far away, on the west side of the Road, somewhere between the hamlets of Skelbrooke and Wrangbrook, there was a Robin Hood's stone, first recorded in 1422 and the earliest known monument to the hero of Barnsdale.

Hathersage and Loxley

Two villages less than ten miles apart claim to contain the grave of Little John and the birthplace of Robin Hood respectively. Hathersage is today a small town on the northern tip of Derbyshire. In its churchyard one can see a 14ft. long grave, surrounded by railings and headed by a tombstone which records it as the last resting place of Little John. The headstone and railings are modern, but there is some evidence to support the claim. For example, the original headstone to the grave is said to be that which stands in the porch of the adjacent church – probably of medieval date and certainly

bearing the much weathered initials L.I. The grave itself was opened in 1784 and an unusually large femur, (thigh bone) was allegedly found within it. The tradition associating Little John with Hathersage is certainly an early one and is recorded in 1652. At that time it was already well known that 'his' bow, hat, arrows and quiver were kept in the church at Hathersage. They were removed in 1729, but the bow was kept in Cannon Hall near Barnsley; a photo of it taken c. 1950 shows a stout weapon some 79in. long. The bow is now kept in Scotland. There is little chance that we shall ever be able to probe more closely into Little John's alleged connections with Hathersage, especially as an adjacent old cottage, claimed to be his last home, was pulled down and completely destroyed in recent times.

On the moors three miles west of Hathersage, (SK 183802) stands Robin Hood's Cross, first mentioned as 'Robins Crosse' in 1319. If it was associated with Robin Hood at such an early date then it would certainly lend support to the connections of this area with the real Robin Hood – but the cross may have been originally named after

(fig. 20) Little John's Cottage
This cottage appeared in a pen and ink drawing around 1830 and shows a cottage at Hathersage, now demolished, allegedly used by Little John in his last years.

some anonymous local person rather than the legendary outlaw.

The village of Loxley, 8 miles north of Hathersage, lays claim to be the birthplace of Robin of Locksley. As early as 1637 it was reported that in Little Haggas Croft could be seen the ruins of the house "where Robin was borne". This is particularly interesting since it was not until Sir Walter Scott wrote Invanhoe in 1820, that Robin Hood was called Robin of Locksley in any known record, be it ballad, book or other document. But the ruins have long since vanished, and again there is little hope that further light will be thrown on either the cottage or the story behind it.

Nottingham Castle – from William The Conqueror to Robin Hood

Nottingham Castle looms large in modern versions of the story of Robin Hood, though it is nowhere specifically mentioned in the earliest surviving tales. It was founded by William the Conqueror, c. 1068, and was at first comprised of an earth mound surmounted by a wooden tower (motte) and a stockade enclosed courtyard (bailey). Although Henry I may have begun the task of rebuilding the castle in stone, it was Henry II who undertook major works here, around 1160. In 1171 he extended the masonry defences to the middle bailey and erected a new stone gate-tower and drawbridge. A Great Hall followed in 1180.

(fig. 21) Robin Hood's Cross
'Robin's Crosse' is first mentioned in 1319, but we cannot be sure that the man who gave his name was the famous *outlaw as Hood was added at a later date.*

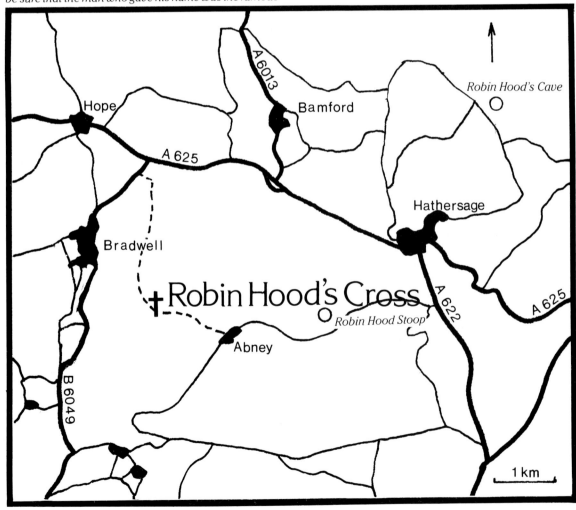

36

Ten years later, while Richard the Lionheart was abroad, Prince John seized the castle and it was held by his supporters until Richard – in a fleeting visit to his kingdom – forced them to surrender in 1194. After he became king in 1199, John spent much time at Nottingham and carried out a lot of new work there. He built a new stone tower in the upper bailey, and re-fortified and extended the outer bailey.

His successor, Henry III, was a frequent visitor to the castle too, and it is in his lifetime that it is possible to place the historical Robin Hood. The building of a stone wall and a gateway "with twin towers" to replace the timber palisade of the outer bailey, between 1252-1255 may have taken place in Robin Hood's lifetime. By this time, the Upper and Middle baileys were packed with halls and chapels as well as stables, barracks and stores.

In the fourteenth century the castle was used as a base for campaigns against the Scots, and it continued to play a major role in British history up until the Civil War. In 1642, Charles I raised his standard here, but the castle was soon seized by the forces of Parliament and subsequently held out against Royalist attempts to retake it. In 1651 it was decreed that the castle be slighted, and following its demolition by gunpowder and pick and shovel, it was finally demolished by the Duke of Newcastle when he built the ducal palace which still stands today.

Nottingham Castle – on the trail of Robin Hood

Although Parliament and then the Duke of Newcastle conspired to totally destroy the old Nottingham Castle, documentary research and modern archaeology have together enabled us to see something of the castle of the time of Robin Hood. If, Robin Hood had become an outlaw, perhaps around 1230 and had later moved his activities from Barnsdale to Sherwood, then he may well have seen the castle of Henry III.

The outer bailey walls, though heavily restored and with the great round tower built by Edward I, still give an impression of what Robin would have seen as he stood in Nottingham town looking up at the great castle. One can still stand in the moat and see the massive round towers which flanked the new gateway built around 1255, and the bridge with a steep pointed arch built at the same time to give

access across the moat to the outer bailey. The drawbridge, which originally ran across the moat from the bridge to the gatehouse, has to be imagined in place of the rounded stone arch of the sixteenth century which replaced it.

Across the space once occupied by the outer bailey, the middle bailey wall and bridge, can still be seen. Built in c. 1170 by Henry I, the stone wall replaced the original timber palisade of the motte and bailey castle. Both it, and the middle bridge were still in use in Robin Hood's time in the thirteenth century. Again, one has to mentally erase the rounded arch of sixteenth century date, and imagine in its place the timber drawbridge resting on the stone abutments and spanning the moat – the line of which is also still clearly visible.

Of the halls and chapels, the barracks and stables, the stores, kitchens, and offices, which crowded into the middle and upper bailey in Robin Hood's time there is, alas, nothing left to see – although King John's kitchen was partially excavated (and covered over again) a few years ago.

Sherwood Forest: 1

Of all the places associated with Robin Hood, Sherwood Forest is the most famous. It provides the backdrop for all the later ballads recounting Robin's adventures and it is his home in all the modern movies about the outlaw. Yet, all the earliest ballads place Robin in Barnsdale, although it is possible that he also operated in Sherwood. Certainly, the change from Barnsdale to Sherwood in the ballads is understandable, for whereas Barnsdale was never a royal forest and in fact was a small, lightly wooded area of no great fame, Sherwood was one of the most famous forests in England.

Sherwood appears in the historical records in 958, where it is called *Sciryuda*. After the Norman conquest and its designation as a royal forest it grew to in excess of 100,000 acres during the twelfth century. Its northern borders were marked by the River Meden, and its western by the River Leen. Although it became smaller in the thirteenth century as estates and farmsteads encroached upon its borders, it was during the period between about 1200 and 1380 that it was most favoured by English kings. This period of course includes the supposed life-time of the original Robin Hood.

(fig. 22) Nottingham Castle
This reconstruction shows how the castle may have appeared in the mid-thirteenth century. Nottingham castle was used as a Royal residence and administrative centre for the county. Robin of Barnsdale would have been outside the jurisdiction of a sheriff based at Nottingham but the northern limits of the county are less than thirty miles from Barnsdale. In the thirteenth century the outer defences were rebuilt in stone.

King John spent much time at Nottingham and consequently hunted in Sherwood on many occasions. His successor, Henry III is known to have hunted in Sherwood only three times in his fifty-six year reign, but the three Edwards who followed him between them made some twenty expeditions to the great forest, and Edward I is believed to have actually held a parliament there in 1290. It may well be the frequent visits of the Edwards to Sherwood that explain why it is that when the king visits Sherwood in the *Gest* he is called Edward.

Sherwood Forest: 2

Within the bounds of Sherwood Forest the most famous spot is that where the Major Oak grows. This massive oak tree has caught the popular imagination, and it has long been known as the place where Robin and his Merry Men held council. Unfortunately, we know this cannot be the case, for the Major Oak is certainly less than 600 years old, probably no more than 500, so that it would not have been even a sapling in Robin's time. Nevertheless, it is well worth a visit, particularly in late Spring when the 'greenwood' is at its best and it is not difficult to imagine 'the men in Lincoln Green' gathered around such a tree.

Of the other places in Sherwood Forest associated in folklore with Robin, few can be shown to have any possible connection with a real Robin Hood. Place-names such as Robin Hood's Cave and Robin Hood's Stable cannot be traced back into the Middle Ages – they are modern attributions. Fountain Dale, south-east of Mansfield, certainly has as much claim to be the home of Friar Tuck as does Fountain's Abbey in Yorkshire, but it is more likely than not that Friar Tuck (like Maid Marian) was a late addition to the band of merry men, put

there by the balladeers; in any case Fountain Dale had no suitable home for a Friar in the mid-thirteenth century. Even more confidently we can dismiss the pretty church at Edwinstowe as the place where Robin and Marian were married for Maid Marian is a post-medieval interloper in the story of Robin Hood.

Two monuments of Robin's period do still survive in Sherwood however. The more impressive is 'King John's Palace' at Clipstone. It was actually built about 1160 (before John was born), and was a hunting lodge used by the king when he was in Sherwood. Henry III, who was probably king in the time of Robin Hood, enlarged the lodge and provided it with a new timber hall, kitchen and chapel. The surviving walls probably belong to further work undertaken by his successor Edward I. At Edwinstowe there is a related earthwork. The Kings' Stand, which was used by royal hunting parties out from the hunting lodge. Foresters drove animals towards the Stand where the king and his party waited with bows at the ready. If Robin Hood did switch his activities from Barnsdale to Sherwood, then he may well have seen both the Stand and the Lodge.

(fig. 23) King John's Palace (Clipstone)
The ragged fragment that stands alone in a ploughed field marks the site of a once large complex including a hall, kitchen, stables and chapel. Henry III was *responsible for the construction of a large timber hall at Clipstone and his son, Edward I built stables to quarter 200 horses.*

LIFE IN THE TIME OF ROBIN HOOD

Knights and Knighthood

Most knights were not the glamorous figures of medieval legend. Initially knights were fighting men, who in wartime provided service and fought on horseback and in peacetime were still expected to undertake service for a certain time each year in duties such as castle guard and escort to important travellers or valuable shipments of goods. For these services they received a Knight's Fee – a grant of land.

By the mid-twelfth century, many knights were already avoiding military service by paying shield money or scutage. At the same time we see the emergence of groups of knights – 'knights of the shire' – who became increasingly involved in jury work and other activities. By the time of Robin Hood (mid-thirteenth century?) knights of the shire were responsible in some cases for overseeing the rights to forest pasture. Such duties, which were unpaid, were time consuming and more and more men refused to take on the burdens of knighthood. Throughout the reign of Henry III, the king was ordering his sheriffs to make sure that all suitably qualified holders of Knight's Fees and all who owned land worth £20, £30 (1282) or £100 (1285) acquired arms, armour and a horse to get themselves knighted. Those who failed to do so were to be fined. It is against such a background that we should view the rather down-trodden figure of Sir Richard of the Lee, who was himself (according to the *Gest*) forced into accepting a knighthood. Nevertheless, the *Gest* also tells us that Sir Richard owned a castle with a wall and double moat, an impressive home for this reluctant knight.

Life in the Castle

We do not know where Sir Richard's castle stood; we cannot identify any Sir Richard of the Lee, let alone his castle. But we can envisage clearly enough what life was like inside a mid-thirteenth century castle. By this time, nearly all castles were built in stone, and defended by high curtain walls, strong gateways, and massive corner towers. The strongest tower usually held living rooms on the upper wooden floors. Such rooms were heated by fires built in great fireplaces set into one wall, and were lighted at night time by candles and oil lamps; in daytime there was often little light in the rooms because their windows were usually narrow slits.

The focus of life in the castle, however, was the great hall, usually built to overlook the inner courtyard or bailey. This was where the men of the castle ate their meals, and where banquets would be held. Colourful hangings would decorate the walls, and the stone floors would be spread with reeds. Whilst the host and his guests ate, they would be entertained by acrobats, jugglers, musicians and balladeers or story-tellers. Meanwhile, in the nearby kitchen there would be great activity as servants stoked the stone ovens, prepared the foods, and turned the roasting spit over the long fire. The records of Nottingham castle report the supplies brought into its stores to subsequently appear on the banqueting tables – wheat, malt, barley, oats, wine, salt, beef, pig and fish. We can compare this with the food in the same stores in the *Gest*, when Little John was servant to the Sheriff – ale and wine, best bread and venison, not to mention the silver dishes, cups and spoons he found in the strong-room.

The Royal Forests

There were dozens of royal forests in Norman England, most of them created by the Norman conquerors. Richard Fitz Nigel who lived in the years around 1160-1190 – perhaps only a few decades before Robin Hood – described a royal forest thus:

"The Kings forest is the safe dwelling place of

(fig. 24) The Thirteenth Century Hall
The poorer knights and squires who tended to become involved in crime would rarely aspire to anything as grand as a castle. The bulk of the lesser nobility inhabited modest manor houses whose defences may have included an insubstantial moat by the end of the thirteenth century. On the lowlands of South Yorkshire such buildings were mostly built of timber and comprised a gathering of small buildings around a barn-like hall.

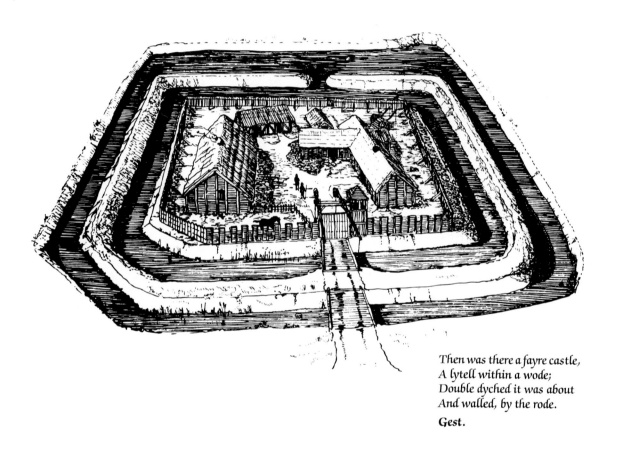

Then was there a fayre castle,
A lytell within a wode;
Double dyched it was about
And walled, by the rode.

Gest.

wild beasts, not of every sort, but of the sort that dwell in the woodlands, not in any sort of place, but in places suitable for that purpose''.

Four hundred years later, it was still possible to talk of royal forests in the same way, even though by that time large parts of the royal forests had disappeared forever:

"A forest is a certain territory of wooded grounds and fruitful pastures, privileged for wild beasts and fowls of forest, chase and warren, to rest and abide there in the safe protection of the king, for his delight and pleasure'' (1598).

So, the purpose of the forest was to provide hunting and game for the king and his followers, and also to provide timber for building, and in some cases for ships. The forests were not areas of unending woodland, however; the royal forests included open glades, wasteland, pastures and villages and fields. What linked all of these areas together was that they were all protected by the Forest Laws, which said precisely what could and could not be

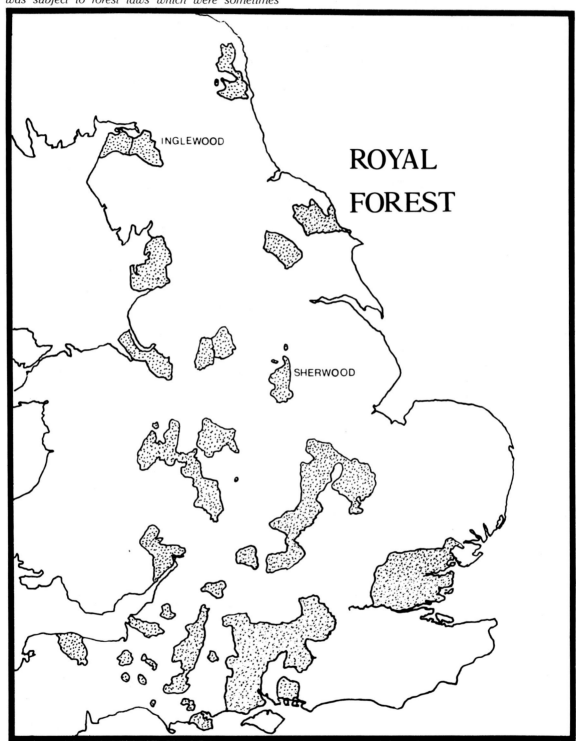

ROYAL

FOREST

INGLEWOOD

SHERWOOD

done in a royal forest, and laid down severe penalties for those who broke the laws.

The Forest Laws

The forest laws were designed to protect both hunting animals and woodland from all but the king and his followers. Offences against 'vert' included cutting down saplings, branches and especially, of course, full grown trees. It was also forbidden to make a hedge, although existing boundaries had to be maintained. Offences against 'venison' including the hunting of red, fallow and roe deer, but also of wild boar. For obvious reasons it was forbidden to carry bows and arrows in a royal forest, or to keep greyhounds. If a forest beast were found dead, then an inquest was held!

The enforcement of the Forest Laws was left to the Chief Forester – responsible for all the royal forests – who was represented in each forest by wardens (or Verders) and foresters. While the foresters saw to the ordinary work of maintaining the forests, the wardens were powerful men. There are many references from the thirteenth century to the extortion practised by these fellows. The Forest

Courts, held every six weeks, could impose such savage penalties that the threat of prosecution was a powerful weapon Until 1217 cutting firewood in a royal forest led to fines, but killing a deer would lead to either death or mutilation. A forest charter issued by Henry II in 1217 reduced the punishment to banishment, which was still a heavy price to pay.

Even in those areas of woodland which were not royal forests, and that would include Robin Hood's Barnsdale, there were often bye-laws preventing the taking of timber and game. In 1395, for example, Wakefield still maintained nine foresters to enforce such bye-laws in adjacent woodland.

Bows and Bowmen

At the very beginning of the *Gest* we find Robin and his companions armed with the longbow, and much is made of Robin's skill as an archer both in the *Gest* and of course in later stories about him. It has been argued that this must place Robin in the late twelfth century at the earliest, for the longbow, it is said, was not introduced into England until that time. Certainly it was only in 1285, after the Welsh

(fig. 26) Hunting the Red Deer
This sketch is taken from a hunting scene produced around 1300 for Sir Richard de Grey who held Codnor Castle in Derbyshire. It is difficult not to see a parallel between this hunting scene showing a man holding the stags head aloft whilst blowing a horn and the death of

Guy of Gisborne. The early story records that Robin killed Guy, cut off his head, stuck it on the end of his bow and announced the death by blowing his victims hunting horn.

43

To se the dere draw to the dale,
And leve the hilles hee
And shadow hem in the leves grene
Under the grene wode

Robin Hood and the Monk

Wars, in which the Welsh had used the weapon to good effect, that Edward I made longbow training compulsory for English yeomen. But the term 'longbow' is rather misleading, suggesting that there was an equally distinctive weapon called the shortbow – which there was not. The bows in use in England were either crossbows or hand-drawn bows. Already, in Matthew Paris's drawings of the batttles of Bouvines (1214) and Sandwich (1217) we see archers pulling powerful bows in the characteristic 'longbow' action – back to the chin. Such weapons were certainly capable of dispatching arrows both fast and hard. Gerald of Wales (late twelfth century) tells us that in his time arrows could pierce oak doors 'a palm's width' thick. Furthermore, it is clear from thirteenth century records that bows were common household belongings at that time, and that they were used above all else for hunting. One such record describes how thirteen men hunted all day in the Forest of Rockingham and with bows and arrows killed three of the deer. Robin's exploits would not have been unusual in the mid-thirteenth century, and we even have testimony, in a West Yorkshire place-name, (Shooter's Hill), that archery butts where archers could practice their skills were already in existence in Robin's home region by the period around 1250. It is worth noting, however, that for all the glamour of the longbow, as a weapon of war it was not valued as highly, even in Robin's day, as was the crossbow. The records of Rhuddlan Castle for 1281 show that whereas crossbowmen were paid 4d a day, ordinary archers received only 2d!

Outlaws in Medieval Legend

There were many outlaws in medieval England, and not surprisingly we find that Robin Hood is neither the only nor the first outlaw to appear in medieval legend.

The earliest of the English outlaw heroes is

44

probably Hereward the Wake. His activities were centred on the Fens, and his enemies were the Normans, in contrast to Robin's location further north and his preoccupation with the church and with the Sheriff. Unlike Robin, Hereward does appear, albeit briefly, in a historical document, for the Anglo-Saxon Chronicle mentions him amongst those who attacked Peterborough in 1070, and he is also mentioned, as a landholder, in the Domesday book.

The same can be said for two further outlaws who lived much nearer to what we believe to be Robin Hood's life-time, during the reign of King John. These were Fulk Fitzwarin and Eustace the Monk. Fitzwarin was a baron, but he nevertheless became an outlaw early in John's reign and he and his band were active far beyond his home district in the Welsh Marches. Eustace, indeed, was a Frenchman but he allied with King John and was given land in Norfolk as a reward. His outlawry was directed largely against his feudal overlord, the Count of Boulogne, but his story nevertheless strikes a familiar chord to readers of the *Gest* of Robin Hood.

The same is true of the stories of two further outlaw gangs of medieval legend. One certainly pre-dates the *Gest* in its surviving form, by some decades. This is the tale of Gamelyn, a younger son deprived of his inheritance, who finally flees to the forest and joins an outlaw gang of which he soon becomes the leader. Eventually, like Robin, Gamelyn is pardoned by the king and is given back his lands. The other famous legend is that of Adam Bell, or the three outlaws of Carlisle. In its earliest surviving form it is roughly a contemporary of Robin Hood, and like Robin, Adam Bell and his associates live in the greenwood and defend themselves with the longbow and the sword. There is one further similarity between Gamelyn, Adam Bell and Robin Hood — none of their exploits are recorded in historical documents.

Outlaws in Medieval History

A variety of medieval documents all present the same picture of outlawry in the period around the time of Robin Hood – bands of felons were active all over England, robbing people at will, kidnapping others and demanding ransoms, ambushing travellers on the highways. Despite their activities such outlaws were often aided and abetted by the local people. We can perhaps get some idea of the

life of Robin Hood and his associates by looking briefly at another gang of outlaws who were active in Derbyshire, Nottinghamshire and Staffordshire, in the early fourteenth century, namely the Coterel gang. The leaders were three brothers James, John and Nicholas Coterel and Roger le Savage.

(fig. 28) The Longbowman
The longbow was a comparatively new weapon in the thirteenth century. Bows were made of elm or yew, often over six foot long, and had a range of over 200 metres.

The story of the Coterel gang has many parallels with the early ballads of Robin Hood. The Coterels were selective in whom they attacked, and were supported by many people, particularly in Derbyshire. They first appear in the records in 1328 when the registrar of Lichfield Cathedral employed them to eject the vicar of Bakewell in Derbyshire. The following year the gang were raiding the chase of Duffield and the parks of Henry of Lancaster in Derbyshire, Staffordshire and Yorkshire.

By 1330 the Coterels had earned considerable notoriety and had established links with another gang in Leicestershire led by the Folvilles. Eustace Folville followed a career of crime from 1326 to 1346 leading a large band of outlaws who killed and robbed almost unhindered. Royal officers were unsuccessful in tracking down the Coterels and the Folvilles, indeed the Folvilles had set upon and killed Roger Belles, a government official and one of the most influential men in the country.

The Coterels had murdered at least two men by the end of 1330 and began a prolonged period of roaming throughout Derbyshire and North Nottinghamshire. During this period the gang continued to recruit followers and moved away from robbing and killing. Their reputation allowed the development of an extensive and successful extortion racket. Sums ranging from one to forty pounds were extracted with little difficulty from rich landowners and merchants.

Local support allowed the Coterels to evade arrest and few members of the gang were brought to justice. Eventually, men from the Coterel and Folville gang found their way into the King's service to fight in foreign wars. Figures of authority had aided and abetted the Coterels, including the Canons of Lichfield Cathedral and the Sheriff of Nottingham and Derbyshire, Sir Richard Ingram.

The Coterels, unlike the Folvilles were Yeomen and thus came from the same class as the Robin Hood of the early ballads. Although the Coterels robbed, killed, kidnapped and extorted money they still could call upon the support of many people. In Bakewell alone nearly 60 villagers were accused of offering support to the gang. The Coterels and their accomplices operated in a society and country which was often corrupt and unjust, and in a land which still had remote and inaccessible regions. Such conditions have led to banditry throughout history and it is against this background that the stories of Robin Hood ought to be viewed if we are to see a reflection of someone other than a legendary figure.

THE ROBIN HOOD TRAIL

The purpose of this section of the book is to provide a selection of places to visit which have Robin Hood associations, either in the ballads, or in legend. They fall into regional groups stretching from Lancashire, Yorkshire, Derbyshire and Nottinghamshire. The sites include historic centres such as York, the evocative woodland glades of Sherwood, Barnsdale, the genesis of our story, and other less familiar places, but all have a special atmosphere to saviour. The motorway network provides ease of access and O.S. maps are useful in helping to locate some sites. In visiting Barnsdale, care must be taken when crossing a difficult section of the A1 (avoiding Robin Hood and his band in the same area would have been less hazardous!) Warm clothing, stout footwear and waterproofs may be needed as medieval buildings and woodlands can be cold and wet places, just as they must have been for outlaws!

1. Robin Hood, The Barnsdale District and Yorkshire.

The area that bears the name Barnsdale today comprises a bleak stretch of open country divided by the A1. In the past the name seems to have been applied to the district between the valley of the Went and the valley of the little brook known as the Skell.

Wentbridge.

The medieval crossing place of the Went, at Wentbridge, has now been bypassed by the main road with the construction of an improved section of the A1. The earliest recorded stories of Robin Hood, as we have seen, make it clear that Robin waylaid travellers on the Great North Road. The Southbound travellers could be seen entering the valley of the River Went from Saylis and as they climbed out of the valley onto the moor of Barnsdale the robbers would have had time to position themselves on the road. The pattern established by Robin Hood was to stop and intimidate travellers to dine with them and extort payment for food and drink. There is no evidence that the area was extensively wooded in medieval times but the steep slopes on either side of the river Went are partly wooded today and no doubt were in the past. It is not difficult to imagine Robin's 'guests' being invited to dine in a secluded wooded place somewhere between Wentbridge and Kirk Smeaton on

the banks of the river before being guided back to the main road after being stripped of their valuables (see fig. 29).

There is a footpath running west from Wentbridge along the valley which allows the visitors imagination to grasp a little of the flavour of the area as it may have been.

(fig 29.)

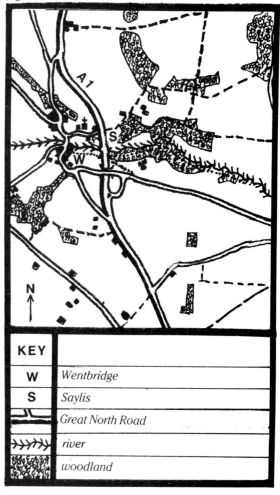

KEY	
W	Wentbridge
S	Saylis
	Great North Road
	river
	woodland

Robin Hood's Well.

An untidy layby formed by an old bend in the A1 marks the site of a once commercially successful stopping place which supported two inns. In the early eighteenth century the well that refreshed travellers was covered by an arched structure which still remains, looking a little forlorn against the background of parked trucks and lorries (see fig. 30).

(fig 30.)

Skelbrooke, Burghwallis and Campsall Churches.

In the small valley of the Skell to the east and the west of Robin Hood's Well are two churches whose origins go back before the Norman Conquest. They were old in the thirteenth century. Unfortunately Skelbrooke church, to the west, was extensively restored in the nineteenth century after a fire, and little of the medieval fabric is visible. Burghwallis is more rewarding for those searching for physical remains from the time of Robin Hood (see fig. 31). Substantial parts of the nave and chancel are Anglo/Saxon in origin whilst the tower has been attributed to the twelfth century although much of the stonework may be earlier. The windows and fittings have been altered at later times but the bowl of the font seems to date from the twelfth century. Campsall has been associated with the Robin Hood tradition as the place according to local legend, of the marriage of Robin Hood. A great deal of the surviving structure stood in the thirteenth century.

Sleep Hill and The Robin Hood Stone.

The site of the boundary guide described as Robin Hood's Stone in a charter copied into the book of charters (cartulary) of Monkbretton priory in 1422 is unknown. It is the earliest record of a certain Robin Hood place name, and the stone lay somewhere in the fields that cover Sleep Hill. The place provides the visitor with the chance to reflect upon the relief of a landscape that would have been familiar to Robin Hood of Barnsdale.

(fig 31.)

Little John's Well.

A short distance from Skelbrooke, upon a junction with the A638 is Little John's Well. A spring still trickles out of a low slope and is contained by stonework that leads the water to a broken cistern (see fig. 32).

(fig 32.)

Pontefract.

Pontefract castle was an administrative centre for the local area and the vast estates of the Lacy Family which included Barnsdale. By the end of the twelfth century it was an impressive complex, with a great hall, chapel and a mass of wooden buildings in the bailey. The importance of the castle helped stimulate the growth of the town which became one of the richest in medieval Yorkshire. The Lacy Family also controlled the estates of the Honour of Clitheroe in Lancashire and their servants, as a result, travelled widely over northern England. The Lancashire connection in the Robin Hood Stories may be a result of the well established links between the Lacy estates based at Pontefract and those at Clitheroe. It seems reasonable to speculate that professional minstrels wrought ballads from anecdotes and tales gathered by the servants of the Lacy Family. The site of the castle still dominates the town and enough of the structure remains to give some impression of its former importance (see fig. 33).

(fig 33.)

49

Sandal Castle (Wakefield District Council).

(fig 34.)

Held by the Warenne Earls of Surrey; a motte and bailey rebuilt in stone in the twelfth and thirteenth centuries. Impressive earthworks have been revealed by excavation.

Conisbrough Castle (English Heritage).

The lords of Conisbrough were the Warenne Earls of Surrey. The Castle was featured in Scott's 'Ivanhoe', and is the most complete medieval castle within a short distance of Barnsdale, and much of the existing structure stood in the mid-thirteenth century. The main feature of the castle is a fine twelfth century round buttressed keep.

2. Robin Hood in Nottinghamshire.

As we have seen it is probable that stories of banditry in Nottinghamshire filtered into the Robin Hood legend at an early date. One of our unlikely candidates for the 'real Robin Hood', Roger Godberd, may have contributed to the extension of the legendary Robin Hood's activities into Nottinghamshire. Roger Godberd led a large outlaw band that murdered and robbed throughout Nottinghamshire between 1267 and 1272. He was eventually tracked down by Reginald de Grey of Codnor and it was discovered that he had at times been harboured by a Robert Foliot, a tenant of the Lacy family. Robert Foliot held land on the edge of Sherwood Forest and land in Yorkshire at Stubbs, Norton and Fenwick. Robert's 'castle' was at Fenwick only five miles from Barnsdale. This connection seems a probable route by which the tales of a Yorkshire outlaw were expanded by the inclusion of adventures in Nottinghamshire.

The numerous Robin Hood place names in Nottinghamshire cannot be traced earlier than 1700, with the exception of those in Nottingham itself. The following sites to visit have more to do with the increased popularity of the legend. With the passage of time Nottinghamshire adopted Robin as their own man, and it is from here that we derive the popular image of the outlaw (see fig. 34).

Nottingham.

As early as 1485 a Robin Hood's close was recorded in Nottingham and by 1500 we find Robin Hood's Well, attesting to early identification with the outlaw by the people of the town.

The castle still has some visible remains from the thirteenth century but most of the surviving structure dates from 1679. The existing medieval work comprises part of the outer defences built during the reign of Henry III. The traditional links with Robin Hood have been reinforced by the erection of a statue of the outlaw on the Castle Lawns.

At the foot of the castle cragg is the Trip to Jerusalem, an inn partly cut into the rock and dated to 1189.

Within the City Council House are a series of frescoes

illustrating episodes from the history of Nottingham which includes a scene depicting Robin Hood as a rather lean elderly gentleman accompanied by a robust and youthful maid Marian.

East of the city centre is St. Ann's Well, once a popular visiting place, as a chair and cap, reputedly Robin Hood's were on display in 1700. In Broadway two windows taken from the medieval St. Mary's church are set into the wall of a warehouse.

Papplewick.

A late tradition asserts that Alan-a-Dale was married at Papplewick church, but little of the medieval structure remains. Perhaps closer to the real world of the medieval outlaw are the grave slabs of the forest wardens. The forest wardens were powerful, and as we have seen tended to extort fines from the local people.

Fountain Dale.

Here is the site of the legendary Friar Tuck's cell, later tradition selects this place as the meeting place of the Friar and Robin Hood.

Blidworth.

Yet another tradition awards this place the mortal remains of Will Scarlet and Robin is supposed to have collected Maid Marian at Blidworth before they went to be married at Edwinstone. A true story from the past of this village, with rather less charm, tells of the arrest of

two men by the Steward of the forest. The men, Robert the Monk and Robert of Alfreton, were held in a building in the village under guard only to be released by a band of twenty men armed with bows and arrows. Eight of the men involved later fled to Yorkshire.

Calverton.

To the north of Nottinghamshire is the village of Calverton which has no traditional association with Robin Hood, but does have a church with a series of Norman panels showing occupations of the local people at different times of the year. It is through such remains that we can get closer to the lives of the people who lived at the time when the stories of Robin Hood were first being told.

Edwinstowe and Sherwood Forest Country Park.

Edwinstowe, set in the heart of Sherwood Forest has been considered a suitable place for the marriage of Robin Hood and Maid Marian. The church of St. Mary's offers little to those searching for medieval Nottinghamshire as it was rebuilt in 1775. Nearby is the Sherwood Forest Park which comprises 450 acres of woodland including, the Major Oak, the oldest oak tree in England (see fig. 35). There are some pleasant and evocative walks in the forest, and an excellent visitors centre.

(fig 35.)

(fig 36.)

Clipstone.

The ruins of the Royal Hunting lodge bear the name 'King Johns' Palace' but the site had been important long before the time of King John and was Anglo/Saxon in origin. Robin Hood stories have been linked to the site but little remains to be seen and the fragments of wall that still stand are in the middle of a ploughed field and so can only be viewed from the road.

Thoresby Hall.

A statue of Robin Hood by one of Madam Tussard's grandsons stands in the forecourt.

3. Robin Hood and the roads to Lancashire.

The links between the Lacy estates based at Pontefract and Clitheroe seems to have been instrumental in bringing a new dimension to the Robin Hood legend. Although the supposed real Robin Hood may have never met a Sir Richard at the Lee of Wyresdale or a Guy of Gisborne the references are at least specific, unlike those relating to Nottinghamshire. The places cited below are worth a visit in their own right, although our concern is how they relate to the Robin Hood legend.

Kirkstall Abbey. (City of Leeds).

The Lacy family were responsible for giving a group of Cistercian monks from Fountains Abbey lands at Barnoldswick. The site proved unsatisfactory and the monks transferred to Kirkstall in 1152 after gaining further land from the vassals of the Lacy's.

Their interests on the other side of the Pennines resulted in the movement of agents of the Abbey through the Aire Gap. Indeed such a large and rich institution as Kirkstall Abbey generated a great deal of traffic on the roads of Northern England and this no doubt accounts for the gifts of a small plot of land and buildings at Wentbridge in 1180. Presumably the holding at Wentbridge was to provide servants of the Abbey with accomodation as they moved along the Great North Road. In veiw of this information it is not unreasonable to suppose that Kirkstall Abbey played an important part in the spread and development of the Robin Hood legend (see fig. 36).

Kirkstall Abbey was dissolved in 1539 but the site was not extensively quarried for dressed stone and the walls of the church and cloister stand to their original height.

Gisburn.

Guy of Gisborne generated his own corpus of stories which were told in the North West of England. He appears in the Robin Hood stories as a villain, a yeoman dressed in a horse hide armed with sword, dagger and bow. This mysterious and formidable enemy of Robin Hood had his roots in the pleasant village of Gisburn (Gisburne before the nineteenth century). Gisburn was a market centre for the local area and in 1260 Henry III granted the monks of nearby Sawley Abbey the right to hold a market every Monday and a three day fair every year. Such grants normally legalised an existing situation. The church is dedicated to St. Mary the Virgin and some of its present fabric dates from the twelfth century. The church had two patrons, the Archbishop of York and the Prioress of Stainfield Nunnery in Lincolnshire.

Clitheroe.

The town and castle of Clitheroe were at the centre of the second great Honour owned by the Lacy family. The Lacy family founded the priory of St. John at Pontefract in 1090 giving land and the tithes of churches that they held. St Johns not only gained tithes from Clitheroe, but also Slaidburn, Colne, Burnley and Whalley. Clearly there must have been a considerable movement of monastic and Lacy servants between Clitheroe and Pontefract. The stories of Guy of Gisburne may well have been linked to those of Robin Hood here, or at Pontefract. The norman keep of Clitheroe castle is unusual as it is so small, nevertheless it still dominates the town (see fig. 37).

Wyresdale and Lee.

It is possible to approach Wyresdale from Clitheroe and Gisburn through the trough of Bowland (possibly the 'pass of Lancashire' in the 'Gest'). At the point where the road from across Bowland meets the River Wyre is the hamlet of Lee, the suspected home of the impoverished knight of the 'Gest' (see fig. 38). It is difficult not to believe the original Sir Richard of the Lee did not come from this place in view of the details given in the 'Gest'.

(fig. 37)

(fig 38.)

53

4. York.

There is so much to see in historic York, and the sites described here were chosen because of their association with the Robin Hood legend. In the centre of the city is Clifford's Tower (English Heritage), built on a motte raised in 1069 by the Normans. The tower was built during the middle years of the thirteenth century (see fig. 39). and is the main surviving section of the large administrative complex of York Castle much of which was demolished in the eighteenth century. It was at the assizes at York, that in 1225 royal justices first heard the case of Robert Hood the fugitive. A fourteenth century candidate for the legendary Sheriff of Nottingham, Sir Henry de Faucumberg, was keeper of York Castle and, Sheriff of the County.

York was also the ecclesiastical centre for the North and the religious institutions possessed extensive estates. Robin Hood the fugitive was a tenant of Archibshop Walter de Grey who completed York Minster's south transept in 1241. A short distance from the Minster are the remains of St. Mary's Abbey. Most of the visible structure was built after the middle of the thirteenth century. Traces of earlier work are still to be found, particularly part of the foundations of the earliest abbey church, and much of the twelfth century gatehouse. (See fig 40.)

The city walls had achieved a length of three miles by the late medieval period, one tower named Frost Tower in 1485, had become Robin Hood's Tower by 1622.

5. Little John and Hathersage.

Hathersage claims to answer the question regarding the ultimate fate of Robin Hood's lieutenant, Little John. Within the porch of Hathersage church is a piece of a thirteenth century tombstone, but as we have seen the initials of Little John seem to have been carved at a later date. The alleged grave of Little John features a fine tombstone erected by the Ancient Order of Foresters. There is more to the story than the tombstone, however, as until the middle of the eighteenth century a bow, arrow, cap and chain armours was kept in the church. This equipment was believed to have belonged to Little John and the bow survives in the possession of a Mr Simon Frazer of Scotland and it perhaps deserves close investigation. It is not beyond the bounds of possibility that an outlaw or fugitive from Barnsdale would find his way to Hathersage in old age. Legend aside the place merits a visit. Robin Hood place names abound in the district including Robin Hood's cross on Abney Moor.

(fig 39.)

(fig 40.)

6. Kirklees Priory and the death of Robin Hood.

It might seem appropriate to end the Robin Hood trail at Kirklees where, according to tradition, Robin met his death after poisoning by the hand of the treacherous prioress. The end is indeed a compelling part of the legend... 'Hold me John while I shoot, and where my arrow falls, there dig me a grave and let me lie' ('Robin Hood', by Henry Gilbert). Unfortunately the supposed grave of Robin Hood, covered by a ruinous monument is overgrown and hidden in the wooded estate of Kirklees Hall. This estate is private property. The site of the priory and its restored gatehouse also come within the private estate (see fig 19.). Nearby is the Three Nuns Inn, built reputedly, on the site of the priory guest house, the name recalling the last three sisters of the priory at the time of the dissolution.

Ordnance Survey Map references of sites related to the early development of the Robin Hood legend.

Place	OS ref.
Barnsdale Bar	*SE 510137*
Blidworth (church)	*SK 585556*
Burghwallis (church)	*SE 537121*
Calverton (church)	*SK 618492*
Campsall (church)	*SE 544141*
Clipstone (hunting lodge)	*SK 604647*
Clitheroe (castle)	*SD 741416*
Conisbrough (castle)	*SK 514989*
Edwinstowe (church)	*SK 625669*
Fenwick (castle)	*SE 582151*
Gisburn (church)	*SD 830489*
Hathersage (church)	*SK 232815*
Kirklees (priory)	*SE 171223*
Kirkstall (abbey)	*SE 259362*
Lee in Wyresdale	*SD 566553*
Little John's Well	*SE 499108*
Major Oak	*SK 621679*
Nottingham Castle	*SK 569395*
Papplewick (church)	*SK 546515*
Pontefract (castle)	*SE 461224*
Robin Hood's Well	*SE 591118*
Saylis	*SE 493173*
Skelbrooke (church)	*SE 511121*
Sleep Hill	*SE 510130*
Steetley (chapel)	*SK 543787*
Thoresby Hall	*SK 638712*
Wakefield	*SE 333208*
Wentbridge	*SE 488173*
York (St. Mary's Abbey)	*SE 598523*

KEY for fig.41 and fig.42

● ●   Major towns and cities.

〜   Main roads (excluding motorways).

⌇   County boundary (pre-1974).

■   Castle.

♙   Monastic site.

▪   Site associated with the Robin Hood legend.

⚐   Chapel/Church.

(fig. 41)

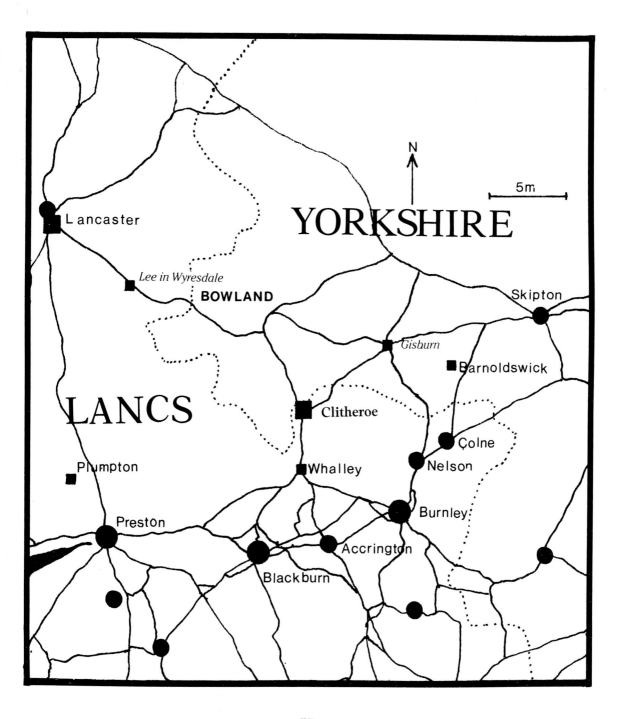

(fig 42.)

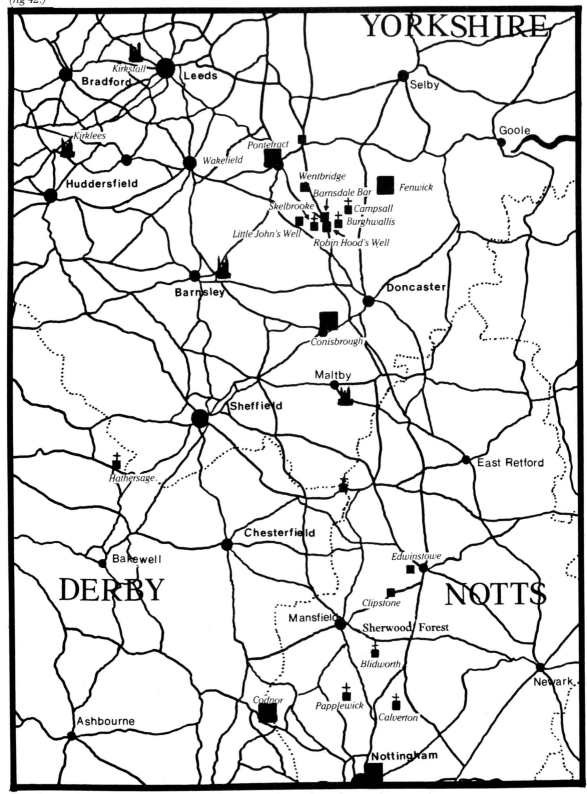

YORKSHIRE

Bradford
Kirkstall
Leeds
Selby
Goole
Kirklees
Huddersfield
Wakefield
Pontefract
Wentbridge
Barnsdale Bar
Fenwick
Skelbrooke
Campsall
Burghwallis
Little John's Well
Robin Hood's Well
Barnsley
Doncaster
Conisbrough
Maltby
Sheffield
East Retford
Hathersage
Chesterfield
Bakewell
Edwinstowe
DERBY
Clipstone
NOTTS
Mansfield
Sherwood Forest
Blidworth
Newark
Codnor
Papplewick
Calverton
Ashbourne
Nottingham

Glossary

Abutment: solid masonry placed to resist the lateral pressure by an arch or vault.

Anglo/Saxon Chronicle: Several sets of annals kept at different monastic houses and written in Early English.

Apse: The semi-circular termination of the chancel or sanctuary of a church at its eastern end.

Ballad: A simple song sung by a balladeer.

Benedictine: Belonging to the order of St. Benedict founded in 529.

Cartulary: A register or collection of documents related to a monastery or church.

Book of Hours: A personal prayerbook.

Chattels: Movable property.

Chase and Warren: Hunting ground, the right to maintain such.

Cistercian: Relates to the monastic order founded in 1098 which took its name from Citeaux in France where their first house stood.

Comely: Pleasing in appearance or behaviour.

Domesday Book: The record of the great survey carried out in 1086 by the order of William the Conquorer.

Curtall: Cut short.

Exchequer: Financial office of the King's household and court.

Feudal: A system of government based upon the relation between superior and vassal arising from holding land in return for services including military obligations.

Gest: Epic poem.

Honour: A lordship comprising many manors or estates.

Justice of the Peace: A person appointed by the Crown responsible for the peace within a certain district.

Knights Fee: Originally an area of land designated to support one knight in the field.

Lincoln Green: A green cloth formerly made at Lincoln and worn by archers.

Mark: Thirteen shillings and four pence.

Minstrels: One of a class of men who lived by singing and reciting.

Palisade: A fence or fortification made of stakes and timber work.

Patron: One who protects and fosters a person, cause or institution.

Registrar: Official keeper of records.

Rolls: Official accounts.

Scutage: A shield tax, money paid in lieu of personal attendance on the lord in time of war.

Sheriff: The King's representative in the shire.

Slighted: Destroyed.

Stanza: A group of rhymed lines.

Statute of Mortmain: This forbade the clergy from gaining more land without the consent of the King.

Tithes: A church tax taking one tenth of the produce in any one year.

Valet: A manservant.

Vert and Venison: The vegetation and the deer which fed on it.

Yeoman: By the thirteenth century the term had come to be used to describe the rich peasantry, they were viewed as a class apart from the bulk of the farming community, as peasant aristocracy. The term yeoman also appears to have been used to describe a servant in a feudal household.

Further Reading

The original ballads.

Dobson R. B. and Taylor J. *'Rymes of Robyn Hood'* Heinemann 1976.
Sheffield J. *'The original Robin Hood'*. J. Sheffield Nottingham 1986.

Historical
Investigation.

Bellamy J. *'Robin Hood, an Historical Enquiry'* Croom Helm 1984.
Harris P. V. *'The Truth About Robin Hood'*. Linney's Macclesfield 1978.
Holt J. C. *'Robin Hood'* Thames and Hudson 1982.
Wiles D. *'The Early Plays of Robin Hood'* D. S. Brewer, Cambridge 1981.

Background Reading.

Hilton R. *'The Decline of Serfdom in Late Medieval England'* Economic History Society 1969.
Keen M. *'The Outlaws of Medieval England'* Routledge & Kegan Paul 1979.
Steen J. *'The Archaeology of Medieval England and Wales'* B.C.A. 1984.

Storybooks.

There are many story books based on the story of Robin Hood. Some of the better ones are:

Fraser A. *'Robin Hood'* (1955).
Gilbert H. *'Robin Hood'* (1912).
Oman C. *'Robin Hood'* (1939).
Trease G. *'Bows Against the Barons'* (1934).
Lancelyn Green R. *'The Adventures of Robin Hood'* (1956).

Typeset by Typebase Ltd., Liverpool.
Printed by Nelson Brothers Limited, Chorley, Lancashire PR7 1EJ.